Contextual Design

Evolved

Synthesis Lectures on Human-Centered Informatics

Editor

John M. Carroll, *Penn State University*

Human-Centered Informatics (HCI) is the intersection of the cultural, the social, the cognitive, and the aesthetic with computing and information technology. It encompasses a huge range of issues, theories, technologies, designs, tools, environments and human experiences in knowledge work, recreation and leisure activity, teaching and learning, and the potpourri of everyday life. The series will publish state-of-the-art syntheses, case studies, and tutorials in key areas. It will share the focus of leading international conferences in HCI.

Contextual Design: Evolved

Karen Holtzblatt and Hugh Beyer

October 2014

Spaces of Interaction, Places for Experience

David Benyon

September 2014

Mobile Interactions in Context: A Designerly Way Toward Digital Ecology

Jesper Kjeldskov

July 2014

Working Together Apart: Collaboration over the Internet

Judith S. Olson, Gary M. Olson

November 2013

Contextual Design: Evolved
Karen Holtzblatt and Hugh Beyer

ISBN: 978-3-031-01079-8   print
ISBN: 978-3-031-02207-4   ebook

DOI 10.1007/978-3-031-02207-4

A Publication in the Springer series
SYNTHESIS LECTURES ON HUMAN-CENTERED INFORMATICS #24

Series Editor: John M. Carroll, Penn State University

Series ISSN   1946-7680 Print   1946-7699 Electronic

Contextual Design

Evolved

Karen Holtzblatt and Hugh Beyer

InContext Enterprises, Inc.

SYNTHESIS LECTURES ON HUMAN-CENTERED INFORMATICS #24

ABSTRACT

Contextual Design is a user-centered design process that uses in-depth field research to drive innovative design. Contextual Design was first invented in 1988 and has since been used in a wide variety of industries and taught in universities all over the world. It is a complete front-end design process rooted in Contextual Inquiry, the widespread, industry-standard field data gathering technique. Contextual Design adds techniques to analyze and present user data, drive ideation from data, design specific product solutions, and iterate those solutions with customers.

In 2013, we overhauled the method to account for the way that technology has radically changed people's lives since the invention of the touchscreen phones and other always-on, always-connected, and always-carried devices. This book describes the new Contextual Design, evolved to help teams design for the way technology now fits into peoples' lives. We briefly describe the steps of the latest version of Contextual Design and show how they create a continual immersion in the world of the user for the purpose of innovative product design.

KEYWORDS

contextual design, CD, HCI, contextual inquiry, field research

Contents

CHAPTER 1

Introduction

Contextual Design is a user-centered design process that uses in-depth field research to drive innovative design. Contextual Design was first invented in 1988 and has since been used in a wide variety of industries and taught in universities all over the world. It is a complete front-end design process rooted in Contextual Inquiry, the widespread, industry-standard field data gathering technique. Contextual Design adds techniques to analyze and present user data, drive ideation from data, design specific product solutions, and iterate those solutions with customers. In 2013, we overhauled the method to account for the way that tech-nology has radically changed people's lives since the invention of the touch-screen phones and other always-on, always-connected, and always-carried devices. This book describes the new Contextual Design, evolved to help teams design for the way technology now fits into peoples' lives.

Contextual Design is a step-by-step process for collecting field data and using it to design any sort of technical product (as first described in *Contextual Design* [1] and then *Rapid Contextual Design* [2]). It has been used to design business systems, websites, mobile devices, mobile apps, medical devices, cloud-based solutions, consumer electronics, automotive electronics, and more. There are three phases to Contextual Design. First, the team immerses itself in the life of individual users through field visits and interprets the data using models to show a big picture of the whole market. Second, the team uses that big picture to drive ideation, inventing new product concepts from the user data. Third, these product concepts are designed with concrete user interfaces and behavior, which are tested and iterated with users. Contextual Design can be used to refine or extend existing products, design for new markets, or drive longer-term product roadmaps. It has been used as part of many requirements and software develop-ment processes, including Agile.

Contextual Design is team-based. It is designed to take advantage of a cross-functional team including such specialties as product management, marketing, product architects, user experience designers (user research and user interface), developers, and service designers, each providing their unique skills and insights to help invent the right solution for users. It builds in ways of involving stakeholders and other team members to assure buy-in from the business and ensure the solution is one the company can successfully deliver. It can then feed into the company's existing development practice. Development practices change over time, but they all need clear design direction*—and that is what Contextual Design provides.

Contextual Design was developed and continues to be driven by the realization that a product is always part of a larger practice, used in the context of other tools and manual processes to make the user's overall life and work. Product design is really about the redesign of the user's work and life, given technological possibilities—designing a new and better way for users to live their lives, achieve their intents, touch the people that matter to them, and perform their activities by introducing better tools and systems. This understanding has only become more compelling as smartphones, tablets, and other devices continue to infiltrate our lives.

Because life and technology are so closely knit, users must be understood in their own context. Usability testing, focus groups, and questionnaires—any data gathering technique with fixed questions and predefined tasks—takes the user out of the context of his or her life. Without the rich context of the user's real life, these methods cannot reveal the most important design issues: the users' motivations, values, emotions, strategies, work-arounds, real-time interruptions and interactions with others, and the constraints imposed by real-world conditions. The core of Contextual Design is to understand users in their own setting, using that understanding to develop deep insight into their lives and applying that insight to a design problem.

---

* Even Agile! Agile Development merely assumes that direction is available from a "customer" role—which is informed by Contextual Design.

This rich data is necessary if the team is to have an accurate, trustworthy basis for driving design thinking, but it's only the first of many *immersion* activities in Contextual Design. That deep, intuitive feeling for the users and their world must be carried through the whole design process and realized in the final product. Therefore, Contextual Design continually re-immerses the team in the data and in the context of users' lives, first in the interviews, then in interpretation sessions, representing users' lives in models, driving innovation from the data, designing to respond to specific issues in the data, and finally, returning to users to iterate and refine proposed solutions.

Continual immersion prevents what we call "design from the I"—designing solutions based on "what I like" or what "seems reasonable to me"—essentially the team designing for themselves. The designer is almost never a good surrogate for the user. They know too much and love technology too much to design for the general public. And they know too little about specific work domains to get the details of a design right. Even a subject matter expert doesn't have the articulated understanding, reflecting broad user experience, that the design team needs. What parts of paying a family's bills are quick and can be done in spare moments on an app—and what parts require heads-down focused attention? What quick questions do medical practitioners need answered right away—and what questions merit in-depth research? Designers cannot get the answers to questions like these right by "design from the I."

The immersion experiences built into Contextual Design make designers "get real" and truly own the complexity of the lives of their users. That keeps designers from the almost inevitable tendency to add features that "might be useful"—a sure signal of over-design. And it ensures that when quick decisions must be made, the designers' intuitive understanding has been tuned through repeated immersion to reflect the users' perspective.

In the rest of this book we will briefly describe the steps of the latest version of Contextual Design and show how they create a continual immersion in the world of the user for the purpose of innovative product design.

CHAPTER 2

Design for Life

Since the late 1980s, the basic idea that designers must understand the context of task activities being supported has stood the test of time. Accordingly, Contextual Design introduced a set of models—diagrams and pictures, each showing one aspect of the users' life context. These original Contextual Design models successfully focused the design effort on understanding the *context of task activity*. They revealed the context of use to identify the structure of the users' activities and the key issues in a market.

These classic Contextual Design models are still relevant; we describe the most important of them below. But since mobile touchscreen devices have become ubiquitous and have fundamentally transformed people's lives, new approaches are needed. Google taught us that any question can be answered, in seconds, anywhere, without arcane query languages. Facebook and Twitter taught us that we can reach out and touch others any time we wish. The iPhone, Android, and tablets taught us that access to our world—our friends, shops, books, news, and pictures, the things we've created and the things we need for work—is always just a touch away. There's no boot time anymore—hardly any setup, login, or preparation. There's just me and my work, me and my life—and increasingly, not much distinction between them.

Given this integration of technology with life, designing technology means *design for life*: designing the details of how to technology works so it fits into all the situations of everyday life. To design for life, we must understand the whole of life as the context of use, which is very different from the context of use of the trad-itional products Contextual Design was designed to create. The wall of separation between home and work has broken down—torn down by people trying to make their whole life work. Tickets to the theatre may be found at work between completing sections of writing or reading or filling out a form. They may be agreed on with text messages during a meeting, and bought later online while on hold during a phone call. A work task may be started over breakfast at home on a tablet, continued at traffic lights during the commute on a touch phone, and wrapped up in the office on a desktop machine. Today, the context of use for what used to be a single, coherent task includes all these places—flowing across place, time, and devices.

Successful design means going far beyond understanding the "cognitive load" or "steps of a task"—buzzwords from a previous generation of user-centered design. Transformative products now help us get our life done and celebrate our accomplishments, connect to the people who matter to us, express the core elements of our identities, and create moments of surprise and sensory delight—all in a product that just works, like magic, with no hassle or learning required. That is a tall order, and means that designers must understand a much wider life context than they ever had to before.

When the iPhone and then Android phones came out, we noticed that the way they integrated into people's lives radically changed from older technology. The language people used was, "This is so *cool!*" We recognized that something fundamental had changed in the way that people related to technology, and we wanted to understand it. So we started our Cool Project in hopes of uncovering the core of the cool user experience.

We went out in the field and talked with more than 60 consumers between 15 and 60 years old about what makes things cool for them. We asked people to show us products with some technical component that they experienced as cool. Then we talked with them about their experience, watched them use the products, and discussed how they transformed their lives. We didn't try to define "cool" for them. Instead, we let them define it by showing us the products they thought were cool. Then we then turned to 30 enterprise workers to see if these same experiences were relevant for workers—and they were. The seven Cool Concepts emerged from our analysis of this data.

Later, we partnered with SAP to develop a way to measure these concepts. The Cool Metric is a set of 40 questions that have been validated with over 2000 people worldwide [3]. The metric can differentiate coolness between different kinds of consumer and business software and between devices. It can be used to compare scores across competitors, or to focus an initial market study. It can be used in between rounds of iteration to see how the team is doing as it develops new product concepts and tests them with users. It works in the lab, in the field, and with a large population survey. Together with the design principles measured by the metric and associated with each Cool Concept we can help our clients move the dial on their product's coolness.

The Cool Project revealed that we must now design for core human motives and the whole of the way an activity fits into life on the go—or what we call the *unstoppable momentum of life*. Therefore, we have had to evolve Contextual Design itself with new data collection techniques, new models to represent the data, new ideation techniques, and new design principles. That evolution is what we describe in this book.

The Cool Concepts are broken into two components. The *Wheel of Joy in Life* organizes the four Cool Concepts that define the way cool products touch our core human motives.

Figure 2.1: The *Wheel of Joy in Life* describes how a product creates joy by enhancing users' lives.

The Cool Concepts we identified from this project are central to understanding what is needed to design for life, and central to designing a product users will experience as cool. The four Cool Concepts of the Wheel of Joy show how products enhance the *joy of life*, how they make our lives richer and more fulfilling:

Accomplishment: Empower users to achieve all the intents of their life, work and personal, wherever they are in whatever amount of time they have, across place, time, and platform. Support the *unstoppable momentum of life* by helping users fill every moment of dead time with useful or amusing activities. Design with the expectation that users will be distracted, splitting their attention across multiple activities. Accomplishment in life is the main driver of the cool experience in the Wheel of Joy in Life.

Connection: Increase the intimacy and collaboration of users' real relationships. Help them make frequent contact, have something mutually valued to talk about and share, and find things to do together as everyone pursues their separate lives. Foster real connection in business relationships as well as personal relationships. Communities of interest—online or in person—will produce real relationships and a sense of connection if they support frequent contact, provide conversational content, and promote shared activities.

Identity: Support users' sense of core self and enable them to express that sense of self in what they do and how they show up to others. Identify the core identity elements associated with the activity being supported by a product and deliver value that increases the users' sense of being their best selves. If people are taking on a new identity, help them create that identity through examples of what others like them do and by checking with friends or trusted colleagues to determine if their behaviors, choices, and values are appropriate. Features that support success in activities core to the person's identity increase the overall value of the product.

Sensation: Provide the user with pleasurable moments of sensual delight through color, sound, movement, and animation. Modern aesthetic design is expected by users today—add appropriate stimulation, graphics, and animation to enhance interaction and create products that evoke a smile. But don't add gratuitous or distracting graphics or animation—that just annoys users and reduces cool. Sensation augments the value of any product, but is the core product focus for games, entertainment systems, music, and sensory-centered product genres.

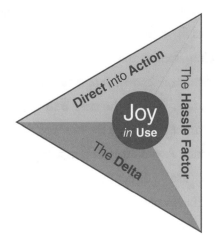

Figure 2.2: The *Triangle of Joy in Use* describes the impact of using the product itself.

The three Cool Concepts of the Triangle of Joy in Use show how the design of the product itself can enhance (or detract from) the *joy of use* by creating moments of "magic" or by eliminating the hassle people have come to expect from technology:

Direct into Action: Provide immediate, simple fulfillment of core intents: I think of what I want, I get the solution—with no thought, no figuring, no deciding. It just happens like magic. Think for me—give me what I want without my having to ask for it, just as Pandora did for music when it first came out. Produce the desired result with little or no direction from me. Of the Cool Concepts in the Triangle of Joy in Use, Direct into Action has the most impact on the user joy in the use of the product. Direct into action calls for much more than good usability and fewer clicks; it calls for true instant into action so that achieving an intent in moments is possible.

The Hassle Factor: Remove all inconveniences, set-up, plugging in, logging in, boxes, customization and technology hassles from the product. Create joy by removing all the glitches and inconveniences that interrupt the flow of life. A "good enough" user experience is no longer good enough. Users no longer tolerate technical hassles and no longer value new function if it is not instant into action. The Hassle Factor combines with Direct into Action in the Cool Metric to create one powerful design focus for creating joy in product use.

The Learning Delta: Reduce the time it takes to learn the tool as close as possible to zero by building on known interaction paradigms and natural interactions like touch and voice. Nudge the user into use with tiny hints. Reduce complexity; reduce the number of things the user has to know and places the user has to go to use the product. Avoid designing in actions and options that increase complexity. Make product use so direct that there's nothing to learn.

This is the age of the ascendency of UX. Good UX and UI design are no longer just nice to have—they can determine whether your product is cool or not, valued or not, bought or not. Even a product that is cool in concept can become uncool if its use is not Direct into Action.

This is as true of business products as it is of commercial products. The term "the consumerization of business products" describes how users' expectations, driven by consumer products, are now affecting their approach to business products. Business products also must be designed for life: fit into the places and times life is lived, support connection to people that matter, enable users' professional identity, and provide appropriate sensory fun.

The insights from the Cool Project require changes to Contextual Design itself. A design team needs to recognize and collect new types of user data on core human motives and behaviors, on wider dimensions of life, and on how the whole of the user's integrated life fits together. So we extended Contextual Design to collect wider data about the whole of life experience, and have added new models to represent this wider view. We also added design principles and ideation activities, all to ensure that the design thinking of the team is focused on the right dimensions of a product to ensure success. Let's now look at Contextual Design evolved.

CHAPTER 3

Field Research:
Data Collection and Interpretation

The first phase of Contextual Design guides a team through gathering field data and interpreting it as a team. By capturing issues and modeling each individual user's experience the team records the data that will later be consolidated to build a coherent view of the practices and experiences of the whole user population. This phase is about getting the best design data while involving and immersing the team in the lives of their users.

3.1   CONTEXTUAL INQUIRY

Gathering requirements for a product is not simply a matter of asking users what they need, like gathering pebbles from a beach. One cannot simply ask for design requirements, in part because people don't know what technology is capable of, but more because most people are not aware of what they really do. The everyday things people do become habitual and unconscious, so they are usually unable to articulate their practices. People can say what they do in general terms and can identify critical problems; they can say what makes them angry with the tools they use. But they usually cannot provide day-to-day details about what they do. They cannot describe inner motivations such as the need to express a particular identity or to feel connected with people they care about. They are likely to forget about the workarounds they had to invent to overcome problems in their current products. This low-level detail of everyday practice is critical to design for life.

Contextual Inquiry, the field data gathering technique of Contextual Design, reveals these unconscious and tacit aspects of life. It guides designers in going out into the field and talking with people about their work and life while observing them. If designers watch people while they engage in their activities, then people do not have to articulate their practices. If they do blow-by-blow retrospective accounts of things that happened in the recent past, people can stick with the details of specific cases using artifacts and reenactments to remind them of what happened. Contextual Inquiry immerses designers in the user's whole life—including those aspects which the user doesn't know how to articulate.

Figure 3.1: Contextual interviews in different life contexts: work, home, and car. Interviews are conducted wherever the activities of interest take place.

3.1.1   RUNNING AN INTERVIEW

Any Contextual Design project starts with a *project focus*. When in the field with the user, designers need to know what to pay attention to—of all the overwhelming detail available, what matters for the design problem at hand? Before starting a project, the team defines the problem to be solved, the users who are affected, the users' activities and tasks that matter, and the situations and locations that are relevant. This project focus extends and refines the core focus on work and life practice given by Contextual Design and the Cool Concepts. It guides how the user interviews are set up and what the designers pay attention to during the interview.

In a Contextual Design project, a cross-functional team carries out the work. Team members conduct field interviews with users wherever they live and work, focusing on the aspects of the practice that matter for the project scope. The typical Contextual Interview lasts 1½–2 hours and is based on four principles that guide how to run the interview:

Context: While people do their life and work activities, observe and discuss what they are doing and why. Use *artifacts*—the things they create or work with—to ground the interview in actual instances. Use *retrospective accounts*—detailed re-telling of specific events in the recent past—to learn about important events that happened outside the interview window. Pay attention to the larger context of life, relationship, and self into which any task fits.

Partnership: Collaborate with users to understand their motivations and strategies; let them lead the interview by doing their own activities and commenting on them. Share the power to direct the interview—the interviewer follows the user's lead and asks about what they are observing. Do not come with planned questions. Instead, use the project focus to guide the conversation towards the most important aspects of their lives.

Interpretation: Determine the meaning of the user's words, emotions, and actions together with the user by sharing your interpretations and letting the user respond—tuning and correcting your understanding along the way. Co-interpret to produce an understanding of how users do the targeted activities, but also how they contribute to their overall life. When immersed in the context of their real life, people will remember what matters. They will not let you mis-construe their motivations.

Focus: Steer the conversation to meaningful topics by paying attention to what falls within project scope and ignoring things that are outside of it. Use insights into life from the Cool Concepts and the Contextual Design models to focus yourself on relevant detail. Let users know the focus so they can steer, too.

A Contextual Interview starts like a conventional interview, with intro-ductions and an overview of the user's situation. At this point we also probe to discover elements of identity important to the user to raise them to awareness and discussion throughout the interview. We then transition to ongoing observation and discussion with the user about that part of the practice that is relevant to the design focus. We watch the user's actions, verbal clues, and body language. We listen for the role of relationships in this activity, collaborations, hassles, and aspects of tools that evoke or reduce joy. We share our insights, understandings, and confusions with users in the moment, inviting the user into a conversation about what is happening, why, and what that implies for any supporting product. As much as possible we keep the user grounded in current activity, but also use artifacts to trigger memories of recent activities. If an interesting event happened in the recent past, we re-tell the story of that event, re-enacting it if possible and using artifacts to help recall details.

Throughout the interview, the Cool Concepts augment the focus of the interview. Each Concept suggests aspects of life that may matter for design. In ad-dition to this general focus, the interviewer guides the user through some directed tasks to reveal key information related to the concepts:

Accomplishment: The interviewer listens for how tasks are split across time, place, and device. If a task is done at the office, is any part of it ever done elsewhere? Research for it done at home? Coordination done with calls from the car? Do users interrupt themselves at points in the task to get a mental break? De-signers can no longer assume that a task is done in one sit-down, focused session.

To see how life and work interleave throughout the day, at some point in the interview the interviewer and user walk through one or more of the user's specific past days, discussing what happened at each point in the day and how the user's technology enabled (or inhibited) doing the tasks of work and life. Interviewers pay special attention to how activities are broken up into chunks of time and get done across platforms and with mobile devices, when the user's attention is split between activities, and the content they access at each point.

Connection: The interviewer always listens for how other people play a part in the user's life and the level of emotional connection the user has with that person. If work or life activities involve collaboration with others the interviewer listens for how that collaboration takes place. In addition, once the interviewer has heard enough to know some of the people important to the target activities, they chart out those relationships with the user (see Figure 3.2). The user talks about how close they feel each person is and what their role is in the activity, and adds additional people as prompted by the discussion. In the remainder of the interview, more people may be added as they come up. The interviewer may also draw small collaboration models (see Figure 3.3) to make the collaboration around a task plain.

Identity: In the introduction, the interviewer probes to understand the user's sense of self relative to the project focus. Throughout the interview, the user may reveal behaviors, values, or accomplishments that they attach pride to or that are important to their sense of self. When this happens, the interviewer raises them up for discussion. Together, they develop a shared understanding of how those experiences reveal an identity element and try to name it. The focus is on finding the sources of pride and self-image relevant to the target activity.

Sensation: The interviewer looks for sensation elements throughout the interview. This usually shows up as an emotional response from the user—a spark of delight or fun or a pause to enjoy an interaction. We even observe users stroking their devices as an expression of their attachment to it. The interviewer talks about what they saw as an emotional response to an element of sensation and lets the user respond.

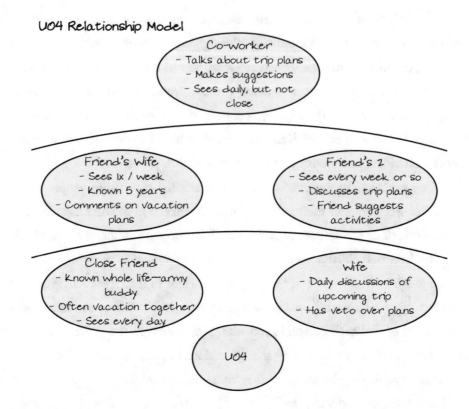

Figure 3.2: Relationship information captured during an interview. "U04" is the user code assigned to the interviewee. Higher layers, farther from the user, show more emotional distance. The interviewer and user worked together to decide where the various people in the user's life should go to illustrate closeness.

The Triangle: Identifying issues raised by the Triangle of Joy in Use requires continual attention throughout the interview. The interviewer watches tool interaction closely to identify issues of Direct into Action and Hassle, and pauses to discuss their impact on the activity and tool experience. They may suggest design ideas to help verify their understanding: "What if the product just gave you that result without your having to ask?" It is relatively easy to see problems and issues—the interviewer may have to look carefully to see what is already working. Capturing what is already direct is important because it allows designer to know what not to change—and how to fix hassles in a way that further supports good aspects of current practice. In the same way, interviewers look for learning issues and complexity and probe them when they find them.

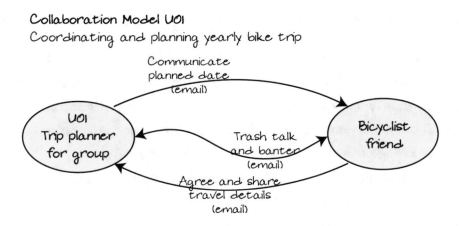

Figure 3.3: Communication model fragment captured during an interview. Such mini-diagrams help clarify the conversation.

Even when designing a business product, it may be useful to discuss the users' interactions with their cool consumer tools. This allows designers to compare business product experience with consumer experience explicitly. The perspective gained in this way provides hints of what a design team might borrow from consumer products that are already valued by their target population.

The fundamental intent of a Contextual Interview is to get design data: low-level, detailed data about the structure of the practice and the use of technology within that practice. Contextual Inquiry, which is based on observing people in the context of their life and work while they do their normal activities, has become standard in the industry as the best way to get this necessary detailed design data. But to design for life we must also understand how the target activity fits into the whole of the person's life and motivations. This has necessitated changes in the structure of the field interview itself, as described above. The result is an interview process that immerses design team members in the details of the tasks users do and also the larger context of emotions, motivations, and fit to life. It immerses the interviewer in the fullness of the user's life so he can embody the user's perspective and represent it to the team.

3.2   INTERPRETATION SESSIONS

The Contextual Interview is the first *immersion experience* of Contextual Design. They immerse a single design team member in the world of the user. The next challenge is to capture that data for use in such a way that it gets incorporated into the mindset of the team. Capturing the data is not the major problem for product teams—having a shared understanding of the world of the user is.

Interpretation sessions are another immersive experience, providing a context for the team to understand the data from a user interview in depth. An interpretation session is a group meeting consisting of the interviewer plus 2–5 team members. Each participant contributes insight from their own unique perspective, leading to a richer understanding of the user than one person alone would have been able to provide. As team members run interviews and participate in interpretation sessions, a shared understanding of the users and the important design issues evolves naturally.

```
T04-14    When planning a trip, one of the
          considerations is whether or not they can
          use their timeshare points.
T04-15    Wherever they go on vacation has to be
          comfortable—and within their budget.
U04-16    Trip planning doesn't excite her husband.
          He gets too stressed out about the budget.
          She likes it, so she does it.
```

Figure 3.4: Interpretation session notes are captured in a document. Each note captures one key point from the interview and is self-contained—it can be understood without reference to the notes on either side.

In an interpretation session, the interviewer tells the story of the interview, using handwritten notes and memory. The interpretation session is conducted within 48 hours of the interview so that the interviewer's memory is still reasonably detailed. Team members ask questions about the interview, drawing out details that the interviewer might have overlooked and indicate what is important to capture. One person acts as recorder, typing notes in a document. Other participants capture Contextual Design models, representing the life and work context of the user. When the discussion sparks design ideas, they are captured in the notes.

The notes are displayed so that everyone can see them. They capture key practice issues, identity and cultural observations, tool and activity successes and breakdowns, task patterns, the use of time, place and different devices, design ideas, and any other issues that have relevance to the project. Later these notes are transferred to sticky notes and used to build the Affinity Diagram.

Simultaneously, other team members capture the structure of the user's activities at work and for life on the Contextual Design models, adding to the model as they hear relevant elements revealed by the interviewer. Each model is a simple representation of one aspect of the user's practice.

The *Day in the Life model* shows the different places in the user's life, the activities undertaken in that place, the devices which support the activities, and the content accessed there.

The *Relationship model* shows the important relationships in the user's life as it relates to the target activity—it's a cleaned up version of the model captured in the interview.

The *Collaboration model* shows each collaboration event discovered during the interview, including who interacted with whom to achieve what and what was shared, done or discussed.

The *Identity model* shows the different observations of sources of pride, self-esteem, and value that emerged during the interview. As the team sees these observations cluster they may start to come up with names for coherent identity elements that are relevant to the project focus.

The *Sequence model* lists the detailed steps the user took to accomplish a task. Multiple sequence models may be captured.

The exact models to capture vary based on project focus. The above models are generally useful, but if the project seeks to support decision making, the team may capture a *Decision Point model*[*] to show the factors working for and against a particular decision. And if a particular physical environment is especially important (such as the interior of a car when analyzing automotive information systems) the team may do a rough sketch of the environment in a *Physical model*.

Capturing these models in the interpretation session make it possible for the team to describe and analyze aspects of the user work practice in a concrete, shared, tangible way. They also automatically teach the design team how to see more when in the field, and this expanded focus helps them avoid overwhelm or focusing only on problems during the field interview.

Because technology has made participating remotely so easy, interpretation sessions may be distributed. Remote participation is a way to involve interested parties who are not local so that they can touch the detailed user experience as it is collected—another immersion opportunity.

Every designer in the room has a job to do, so each has to process the data and think about its implications. This combination of listening, inquiring, thinking, and drawing or writing the implications creates the immersion in the data that results in real understanding and insight. By the end of the interpretation session, all participants "own" the data and have incorporated it into their view of the user and the project.

---

[*] The Decision Point model is a variant of Contextual Design's original Cultural model. We find this useful for products looking at buying or choosing as a primary focus. The Artifact model may still be useful, but as paper artifacts were transformed and put online over the years we find that use of this model became rare.

CHAPTER 4

Consolidation and Ideation:
The Bridge to Design

In the first part of Contextual Design, teams collect in-depth field data about all relevant parts of their customer's lives. But the purpose of collecting data is to use it in making design decisions and inventing products. Helping a diverse design team take the data produced by researchers and use it for design remains one of the biggest challenges of our industry.

At this writing, Contextual Inquiry has been taught in school for well over a decade; UX groups are now a standard part of technology companies. But the creation of UX groups tasked with research means that all the insight and deep knowledge about users tends to be locked in that group. Transferring not just knowledge but insight, understanding, and a "feel" for the user's world is the first step in creating a bridge between data and design. One of the greatest challenges for UX professionals is how to drive data into the ideation process; how to ensure that the lives of the users actually impact design thinking in the large.

Lives are complex and detailed, so sharing the findings of a field study can be challenging. Taking all that data in can overwhelm team members and stake-holders alike. Management often tries to simplify the problem by asking for the "top 10" problems or features, which makes the data easier to deal with but also limits the impact—the only way to make real change is by rethinking the problem. If rich customer data won't be used because it's too overwhelming to deal with it, why gather it at all? And in fact, some companies do abandon that goal, and with it the possibility of a more transformative product.

But even a smaller, more targeted project scope benefits from rich data. A "usability release" which tries to fix all the hassle in a product requires a more comprehensive approach to understanding the customer's world, because hassle comes from a bad fit between the product and the users' lives. Design for the next release of an existing product is still best served by understanding the activities and lives of the target customers holistically so that the next release can make the most impact.

Effective design depends on the UX professional's ability to communicate the customer data and insights in a way that is consumable and relevant for the people in the design process. *Communication design*, the intentional creation of artifacts that communicate the data, is a necessary design step and an important skill for all UX professionals [4]. Communication design is built into this part of Contextual Design, the bridge from data to design action. Communication design has its own set of principles that make it work; we'll illustrate them below.

The graphical models of Contextual Design are designed to help people internalize the world of their users. Design teams have always been able to walk the Affinity Diagram and use Sequence models to drive design. But some of the other models in Contextual Design, like the Flow model, are more difficult to build and use. So when we set out to design new models like the Day-in-the-Life Model, which represents how devices, place, and time are used in life, we took a step back to re-think how we present this complex data so that it can be consumed by teams easily. The new Contextual Design models described below have been created and iterated to ensure that they work well as a bridge to design.

Along with the models, we use a facilitated workshop to guide the team through using the data for generating new product concepts. These workshops create another immersion experience for the team. Interviews and interpretation sessions immersed researchers (and helpers) in the lives of users; now the rest of the product team needs to be immersed in the data as well. When the team does a *Wall Walk* of the consolidated data they steep themselves in the world of the user. Then with this knowledge the *Visioning Session* leads a team through group story-telling that embodies new product concepts. Together, they form a reliable bridge to design that has stood the test of time.

With the introduction of the Cool Concepts we have added a second workshop, the *Cool Drilldown*. In these four days the team further refines the initial product concepts using the design principles associated with each Cool Concept.

As with the Visioning session, in the Cool Drilldown each sub-team goes back to the user data before pushing the product concept further based on cool principles.

Since both workshops continuously use and reuse the consolidated data, the team practices making the bridge from data to design and internalizes the data as they do so. Our work with teams has shown that these three steps are extremely effective in producing an initial set of market-relevant, transformative product concepts which can then be defined and validated in more detail.

Below we describe the consolidation process and show examples of model communication. Then we describe the steps of ideation used in Contextual Design.

4.1   DATA CONSOLIDATION

Products serve whole markets, but we can only find out about users by talking to them one on one. Consolidation is the step that brings the data from all users to-gether into a single, coherent view, showing common patterns without losing the key variation across customers. Consolidation produces a representation of the market that drives design action, but acts as an immersion experience itself—team members who participate in consolidating the data interact with it intimately and become very familiar with it.

Quantitative techniques make data manageable through *data reduction—* looking just for the top findings, which hides the richness of the actual data. Contextual Design takes a different approach: organize the rich, detailed data to reveal the key issues, basic structure of work and life practice, and see patterns across a market. The process of organizing the complexity of life so designers can use it is greatly helped by having multiple ways to represent different aspects of life. The Contextual Design models represent different points of view on the life, the behaviors, the structure of the practice, the motives, and the issues of the tar-get population. The Affinity Diagram reveals the overall issues of the market; the Day-in-the Life model shows the structure and movement of the users as they get relevant activities done throughout the day. These are both big-picture models that reveal the larger world the user lives in. The Sequence model shows a lower level view of particular tasks, and the Collaboration model shows group-level coordination and roles. These are more detailed models. The Identity, Relationship, and Sensation models reveal targeted customer motives, feelings, and values. Each model focuses the team on one point of view of the user's experience.

Contextual Design's multiple models allow the rich field data to be structured into multiple views so that complexity is manageable. Each model shows different points of view on the user's world—points of view that we have found to be particularly helpful for driving design thinking. Once consolidated, the team can see what is going on in their market from each perspective and derive insight. Then they can design the best way to represent that data so that it will drive ideation. *Communication design*—the intentional creation of diagrams and pictures to communicate data—is an essential skill. Good communication design ensures that the data and its insights can be used by the team to drive innovation.

Figure 4.1: Using the team room to create an immersive experience.

4.1.1   THE AFFINITY DIAGRAM

The process of consolidation is easiest to see in building the Affinity Diagram, but it is similar for all models. To build the Affinity, all interpretation session notes from all users are printed on sticky notes in random order. Then the team arranges the notes in a facilitated process that takes two or three days depending on the number of notes and the size of the team. The notes are grouped on a wall to reveal distinctions relevant to the design problem: each grouping describes a single issue or a point. Groups are kept small, four to six notes in a group. When there is a lot of data on a point, this forces the team to find more groups and therefore more issues and more insights. Groups are not predefined—they emerge from the data and are specific to the data. Finally, the groups are labeled with blue sticky notes to characterize the point made by the group. The blue labels are then organized into larger areas of interest under pink labels, and the pink labels are grouped under green labels to show whole themes.

Building the Affinity forces the team members to deal with each specific observation from the field data and think about what it tells them about the user's world. Assigning this activity to one or even two people would be overwhelming, but building it as a team over a few days is manageable and provides another immersion experience. Building the data is already a bridge to the design process.

The affinity is built from the bottom up, grouping notes into themes one at a time. The result is a single hierarchical structure that tells the story of the issues across the whole user population when read from the top down. The final affinity is easy to read and interpret—a designer can simply read through it like a story, starting with a green and then reading down through the pinks and blues, sampling individual notes to get a full picture of the data. If done right, a design team can understand all that matters for the market simply by reading the labels. The affinity structure simplifies the complexity of the data without losing the rich detail which is still available in the individual notes.

The Affinity Diagram is a good example of effective communication design. It presents a *meaningful structure*, our first principle of communication design. The hierarchical structure is familiar to everyone and naturally chunks lots of data into smaller groupings; groupings represent coherent themes and contain yet smaller chunks, each of which can be consumed one at a time. The resulting structure is easy to read, rendering the complexity of field data consumable.

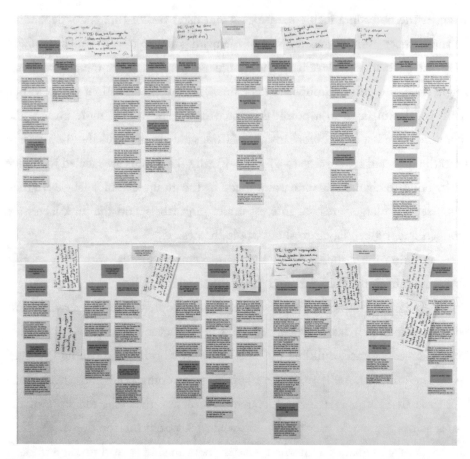

Figure 4.2: An Affinity Diagram during construction, showing how notes and pictures from individual interviews (the yellow notes) are grouped into a hierarchical structure (the blue, pink, and green notes). Note that photos taken during interviews are integrated into the affinity wherever appropriate.

The group labels are written in *story language*, from the point of view of the user talking directly to the team. This is our second principle of communication design. Humans are storytellers. User data that is expressed as story can be read and understood intuitively. The reader is hooked in emotionally as well as intellectually. This makes the communication more direct, immediate, and impactful. Stories create a visceral experience making the user's world real to the designers—and so more likely to stimulate design ideas.

Story language presented within a meaningful structure provides designers a *way in* to the user data, our third principle of communication design. If designers have no way in, they can't design for the data—they can't see the relevance. Part of communication design is designing this way in. Others have addressed the same problem with games, competitions, or cartoons to engage the design team. We prefer to build the design thinking stimulus right into the model itself.

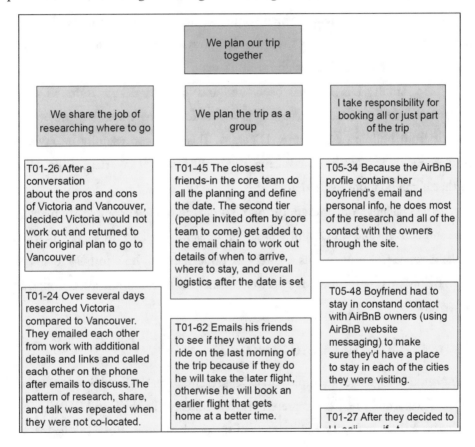

Figure 4.3: A section of Affinity after it has been put online, showing how yellow sticky notes from individual interviews group into blues and pinks revealing issues and themes. Note that the blues and pinks are written in the voice of the user.

Finally, the Affinity supports *interaction* with the data. The Affinity *Wall Walk* (described below) encourages designers to engage with and interact with the data. Interaction is important: any presentation of the data that lets the team get away with being passive and receptive will not help the team go from the data to design. To truly incorporate new information, people need to manipulate it and interact with it in ways that stimulate design ideas.

The Affinity is a model of good communication design (which is why it is so popular): the structure chunks relevant themes into manageable sections which lead the team through the data; the story language in the labels and individual notes evokes users' experience, which stimulates design ideas relevant to the point of view of the model. Together, they give designers a way in to understand the data and to interact with it with design implications.

The Affinity Diagram has been used and loved by design teams as a way to capture information and present it to others for a long time. Any project will benefit from building an Affinity Diagram. This data can usefully be revisited throughout the project, by other teams, and in the future. It's worth putting online so that it can be more easily shared.

The challenge of communicating field data is to make complexity manageable and consumable. The Affinity Diagram does this well, so the elements which make it successful provided us a guide for understanding how to help teams use data. Below we discuss how we used these principles of communication design for other models.

4.2   CONTEXTUAL DESIGN MODELS

Contextual Design uses multiple parallel representations to show different aspects of users' work and life. Each representation is coherent in itself, and the team can look across them to see the full richness of the user's practice. The thinking process used to build the Affinity Diagram is the pattern for all model consolidations: first break individual observations into meaningful, self-contained parts; then organize those parts to reveal themes and the structure of the practice appropriate to the point of view of the model; finally represent the themes in a way that can be easily consumed by a design team, ensuring that the most important insights are accessible. Here's a quick look at some of the primary models of Contextual Design and how they are consolidated.

The Day in the Life model (Figure 4.4) is brought together to show the overall structure of users' days and how work and home tasks fit into time throughout the day, supported by mobile and non-mobile technology. To recognize the common pattern across users for the this model, the observations that matter are the small, focused activities which occur throughout the day in different places, at different times, on different platforms, which work together to get larger activities done.

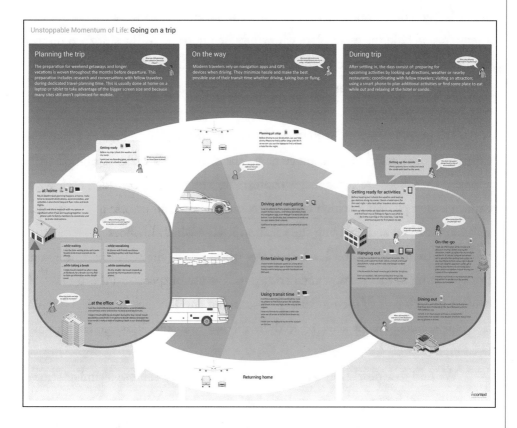

Figure 4.4: A full Day in the Life model. This model shows the three primary areas of interest for travel—at home and work prior to the trip, getting to the vacation location, and activities during the trip itself. Activities, issues, and device use are shown in each location.

For example, when studying travel planning, the team saw a user pass the time waiting for her son's swim lesson to be over by researching possible destinations on her iPhone. This is a small, self-contained activity, easy to interrupt and easy to pick up again, which might happen at many points throughout the day. It was brought together with other occasions of quick research done while waiting. Looking at the part of the model shown in Figure 4.5, this insight is represented as a rectangle within the orange home bubble labeled "...*while waiting.*" This shows that one key part of travel planning happens at moments, with partial attention, and may be interrupted at any time. Any design should support this context of use by being quick to pick up and get into, simple enough to work despite partial attention, and hold the user's place when they are interrupted. The story text on the model captures the essence of the user exper-ience. The model does not attempt to cover all instances observed—instead, it provides a characteristic example to communicate the behavior.

The overall structure of the Day in the Life model is designed to evoke the experience of time, place, and movement. The grey panels make it immediately apparent that there are three major contexts for the team to consider, each with its own issues: planning, which takes place around home and work; getting to the vacation location; and enjoying the vacation itself—which includes planning and research, although at a lower level. The large white arrows show that there is a flow from planning to the location and back again. The use of space and the amount of content in each part of the model makes scanning and focusing possible. Graphic elements are deliberately selected to draw the eye to distinctions the team wants to communicate.

We find that nearly any kind of work or life activity can use a similar struc-ture, with modifications based on the exact situation. The big cycle represented by the white arrows show the flow through the day; the place and time contexts represented by the gray panels might be home, work, and third places (offsite meetings, coffee shops, and so forth).

The text blocks on the model present the users' lived experience, highlight-ing key issues in small, easy-to-consume chunks. Each chunk can be scanned in a moment and invites reflection right then on what the design might do to respond to this issue. They are presented in personal, story language—Figure 4.5 shows one part of the planning phase, including doing research during the son's swim lesson mentioned above. This vignette from the actual data makes the data real and helps the designer connect to the experience represented by the model at an emotional and intuitive level.

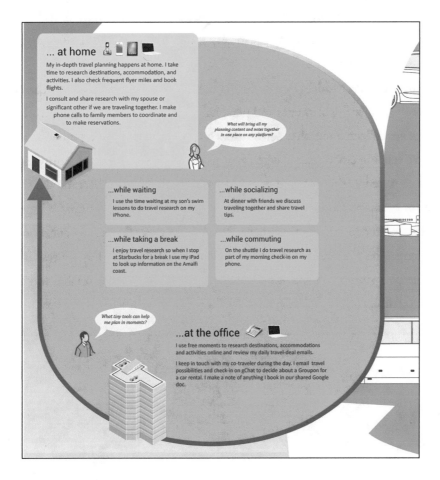

Figure 4.5: A portion of a Day in the Life model showing how travel planning fits into life, in different locations and on a range of devices.

Our principles of communication design say that designers need a way in to the data. To provide direct stimulus for design thinking many of the Contextual Design models, including the Day in the Life, use small speech bubbles scattered around the diagram to ask direct questions of the reader. These questions give designers an initial focus when looking at the model—an entry point for thinking about the implications of the data, highlighting what the team thinks matters to the design. From there, designers can jump off to thinking about other implications—and they can ignore the questions entirely if they wish. But the question bubbles stand as an example of how to use the data. We have found that the simple addition of these questions has drastically increased the number of design ideas generated for each model.[*]

The Identity Model (Figure 4.6) is built using a similar process. The observations about identity elements and personal values captured during interpretation sessions are collected together across users into potential identity elements: sources of pride, self-esteem, or value as relevant to a target activity. Any identity element names captured during interviews and interpretation sessions become the starting point for grouping the observations meaningfully to represent different aspects of self that matter for the project focus. Then, looking at the whole collection, the team agrees on the important identity elements and what they represent. They pick the best stories to express this inner experience in a consumable way to the design team.

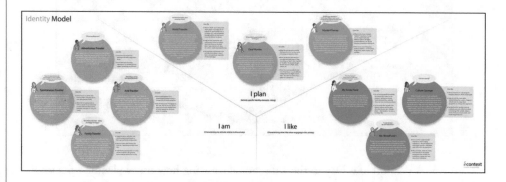

Figure 4.6: A full Identity model for travel showing the three sections "I am", "I plan", and "I like"

---

[*] The final design of each of the graphics for the Contextual Design models was iterated with users in Visioning Sessions. After their early use we talked about what worked and didn't, where participants were confused, and what models prompted the most design ideas. The structures of the models we present as a standard part of Contextual Design have stood the test of successful use.

Each identity element is given a descriptive name and a short summary, written as a story from the point of view of the user (Figure 4.7). Each identity element is also given two ways in to understand the implications. The first is a *catchphrase*, written as though spoken by the user, summarizing the emotion around that element. These catchphrases help designers relate to the inner experience of the user. They point to a feeling the designers may recognize in themselves and be able to resonate with. Second, we add *Give Me's* to the model. These are design ideas generated during consolidation. They may or may not be used in the final design, but are offered in the "Give me" box to make the link between data and design explicit and to act as starting points for the designer's own creativity.

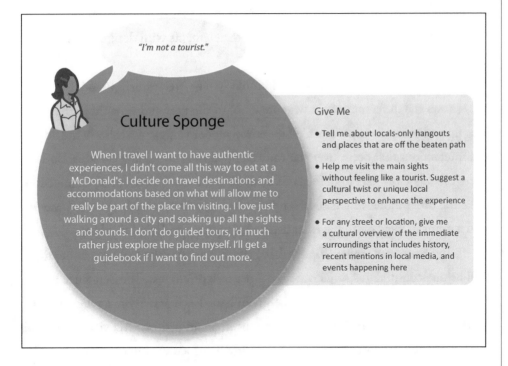

Figure 4.7: One identity element from the travel Identity model. The "Give Me" design ideas act as starting points for the team's own design thinking.

Once identified, similar identity elements are grouped together into sections. The sections vary by project, showing how the user sees themselves in relation to the activities addressed by the project. In Figure 4.6, "I plan" represents identity elements specific to the planning activity; "I am" represents identity elements that reveal an overarching approach to travel; and "I like" represents what is desired during the trip itself.

From a communication design perspective, the largest structure of the Identity model is the sections inviting systematic exploration of a small set of identity elements; each element represents an identity theme with a name that is evocative and is described in story text; and the catchphrase and "Give Me's" provide a way in to start design thinking.

As a representation of a market, the Identity model has proven very powerful for teams. It helps them understand who their users are in a way that is immediately actionable. And because any one person in a market may manifest any number of identity elements, addressing all the elements with design ideas ensures that the market as a whole is covered.

Other models are consolidated similarly. **The Relationship model** (Figure 4.8) shows the different people who are close to the user and how they affect setting up and going on trips. **The Collaboration model** (Figure 4.9) shows the different interactions that occur over the course of planning and going on trips. Both of these models show data to help teams design for the Cool Concept of Connection. Like the other models their representation has structure, story language, a way in, and a point of view on the lives of users that matter for design thinking.

The **Sequence model** (Figure 4.10) shows how specific tasks are done; there will be one consolidated sequence model per task of interest. The Sequence model is broken into *activities*, set off by the green bars. Each activity is a coherent part of the overall task with its own set of concerns and actions. Activities are good candidates for support in an app, being smaller, focused intents that could be supported with a targeted set of functions. Sequences also show *intents*—the pink boxes—which say why the user cares about doing a step. Intents guide redesign by showing what really matters to the user—as long as core intents are supported, the

---

* The Collaboration model is a graphical communication of the interactions of a workgroup or any set of people working together to get things done. It is the evolution of Contextual Design's original Flow model designed for communication. We generally restrict use of the Flow model to large processes; the Collaboration model is more appropriate for most activities.

steps can be changed. Finally, *breakdowns*—the boxes marked with red zigzags—show problems that should be solved in a redesign. The Sequence Model has a classic linear structure, but the activities break it into manageable chunks and the breakdowns and intents provide a way in.

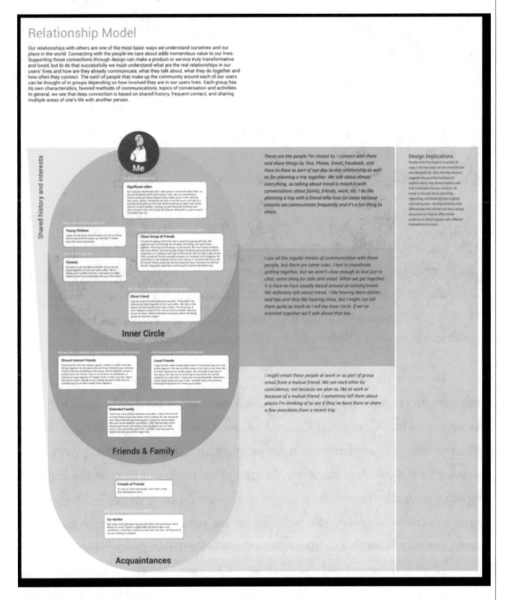

Figure 4.8: A Relationship model for travel, showing the important people involved in the travel story and how close they are to the user.

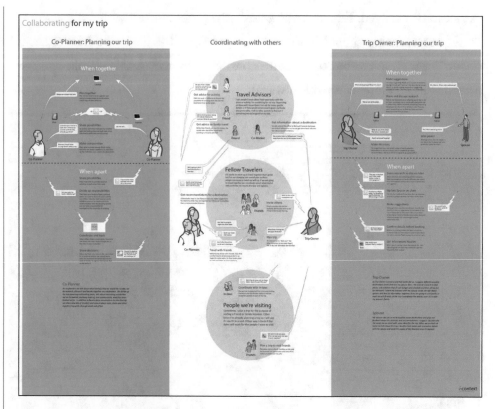

Figure 4.9: A Collaboration model for travel. The yellow sticky notes attached to the model are the result of a Wall Walk, described in the next section.

Personas are treated as part of consolidation in Contextual Design. (Personas were first described by Cooper in *The Inmates are Running the Asylum* [4] and incorporated into Contextual Design in *Rapid Contextual Design*.) Personas are an effective way to characterize users for people who did not go on field visits. They also act as a convenient summary for designers, putting a face on the different types of users they must satisfy. They can act as a focusing device—the team can agree to concentrate on certain personas for the current project. Personas, like the new Contextual Design models, communicate information through story—catchy, personal, with the emotional element built in. Because they are based on field data, they have the depth and richness of real user experience behind them. But because they are presented as individual stories, they are simple to comprehend. We find that personas tend to spark fewer design ideas than the models, but they are fa-

miliar and serve as a good starting point for understanding who was interviewed
by the team.

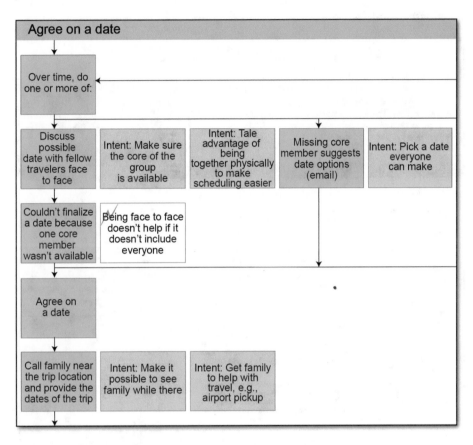

Figure 4.10: One part of a consolidated Sequence model showing how people plan for
travel. Note the multiple branches, showing different possibilities found in the actual data.

The Sensation model is treated a little differently because it helps guide visual
and industrial designers in the overall aesthetic of the product rather than defining what the product should do. Our experience with these designers shows
that they can more easily design for an overarching emotional experience if
they have a visual stimulus and a list of key focusing words rather than a text-
heavy model. Traditionally, visual and industrial designers create a set of words
and pictures which communicate the overall feeling and emotional experience
the product is supposed to create. Often these "mood boards" are created by

teams generating words based on a brand goal or their own ideas. The Sensation model is a data-based mood board built using similar principles as the other consolidated models.

Figure 4.11: A persona developed during the Cool Project characterizing one type of mobile device user. All information in the persona was collected during user interviews.

A Sensation model is created by walking the user data looking for evocative words, user quotes and implied emotional experience and desires associated with the target activity. These observations are gathered from the consolidated Affinity and other models, ensuring that the Sensation model represents the experience of the market. Then the quotes and words are organized into themes and combined with images that evoke each theme. The images are chosen to be emotionally evocative of the experience desired by users and the words are chosen to express that experience. Together they provide the way in for the aesthetic designers. All is then assembled into the final Sensation model that shows the experience in images.

Figure 4.12: Full Sensation model showing the different aspects of sensation that affect the travel experience.

Consolidation is a way to organize and present complicated field data so that it can be used to drive design thinking. The consolidation process of collecting, organizing, structuring, and naming themes and significant findings gives UX professionals and design teams another immersion experience—and the beginnings of the insights that are important for the design. Creating the models for communication helps hone and focus the insights and the messages. The presentation itself is a critical step in creating a bridge from data to design. This is the necessary first step in the ideation process—getting the evocative data ready to help stimulate design thinking.

Figure 4.13: One panel from a Sensation model for travel showing one aspect of sensation. The images are chosen to communicate the emotional experience of travelers in ways words cannot.

Consolidated models are a lasting representation of the user's world and market needs. They are a corporate resource—they can be used, accessed, and updated over and over. We have found that the basic structure and intents of life represented in consolidated data do not change much over time—unless the industry is undergoing massive disruption.[*] New technology usually just changes the details of how those intents are accomplished. A company can expect to use this kind of data for 3–5 years across multiple product rollouts.

When graphical Contextual Design models are used with the Affinity Diagram and Sequences, we have found that they successfully shift a team's invention

---

[*] Industries undergoing "disintermediation", such as publishing, experience such major disruption. Major platform changes such as that introduced by the iPhone also cause such disruption.

in the direction suggested by the Cool Concepts. They truly form a bridge to invention and a way to bring the team into a shared understanding of the users' world and so to the best design solution for their company.

4.3   IDEATION

The problem of design is not just that of specifying a technical system—it is the reinvention of life, from the most global elements to the most detailed. New technology changes how people approach their work and how they live their lives; that is why it is attractive. A Design for Life perspective ensures that those changes are desirable and valued by users.

To do such design successfully, designers need a deep understanding of the life of the users so that their re-invention of life will be valued. The goal of "disruptive technology" is to transform life in a desirable direction for people—not to disrupt the ability to get life done enjoyably! For great designers, immersion in users' lives has always been the trigger for creative, new invention. The details of life—core motives, life structures, challenges, issues, problems, desires, and so on—feed design action.

But this is only true if the designers know what technology can do. They need to be masters of the *materials of design* for their domain. User data may provide the inspiration, but it is the materials of design that are used and recombined to create something transformative. The materials of design include everything that can be brought to bear on the problem. Knowledge of apps, responsive design for different screen sizes, appropriate paradigms for presenting information and functions on different devices, use of location information, tracking user actions, active learning, machine learning, accessing cloud data to make the users' data available, UI layouts and graphic design trends—these are just some of the materials of design necessary for successful products today.

When technology changes—as it did with the introduction of the window/mouse interface, and again with the Web, and again with touchscreens on smartphones—the materials of design change too. Designers have to re-learn the materials to stay current. As a community, we also invent new materials and expectations for what is modern. Whereas once a tree structure UI was innovative, it became dated and old. Whereas users once expected to fill out forms to tell applications their preferences, today they expect products to figure out what they want through their actions. Without a thorough grounding in the materials of design at every level, designers cannot create appropriate products for their markets; they must have these ideas and concepts at their fingertips while they are immersed in the users' world so that they can respond creatively with invention, while building on modern standards.

Contextual Design supports ideation through two team-based workshops: the *Visioning Workshop* (3 days) and the *Cool Drilldown Workshop* (3–4 days). Together, they form a facilitated process for immersing teams in the users' world by walking them through the consolidated data, generating scenarios exploring how technology can enhance users' life and work, and driving the implications of the Cool Concepts into the emerging product concepts. These workshops assume that the participants know their materials—if not, you may need to run pre-workshop sessions to educate participants. These workshops produce innovative product concepts honed by the Cool Concepts, delivering a modern experience that enables technology to transform daily life for the better.

4.3.1   THE VISIONING WORKSHOP

The Wall Walk. The first step in the Visioning Workshop is the **Wall Walk** in which participants, whether they were involved in data collection and consol-idation or not, immerse themselves in the data in preparation for design. The goal is to help designers link design ideas to the data—the real structure and challenges of the users' world.

In the Wall Walk, the facilitator introduces the project and each step of the process to the group, which can include stakeholders who learn about the data and inform the direction of the vision team. If personas were created, the first step is to introduce them so that everyone has a sense of who the users are and what their goals are. Then the whole group walks the Affinity Diagram, placing sticky notes with design ideas directly on the data displayed on the wall.

The Wall Walk is an individual, silent experience. Each person reads the Affinity Diagram like a story, top-down. Each top-level section of the Affinity communicates an issue through the language of the green label; lower-level labels present the organized user data with detail about the issue. Each team member thinks about design implications and writes design ideas on sticky notes, posting them next to the data in the Affinity they are responding to. As they read and respond to more and more individual issues, the designer's ideas naturally get more holistic and complete. This interactive process of reading, writing, and posting grounds designers in the users' practice and helps them make the leap from facts about the work to design implications for the product. This interactive step of the Wall Walk starts to pull designers across the bridge from data to design.

After walking the Affinity the facilitator makes a list of the issues that the group thinks must be addressed to have a successful product. Anyone with an issue voices it and it is captured. In this way the group hears what matters to each other, creating a shared understanding in moments. Following this, the facilitator captures a list of *hot ideas*: design ideas that have the potential to spark a holistic solution. Hot ideas are written on a flip chart and grouped by the facilitator into themes that can be used as starting points for the visioning session.

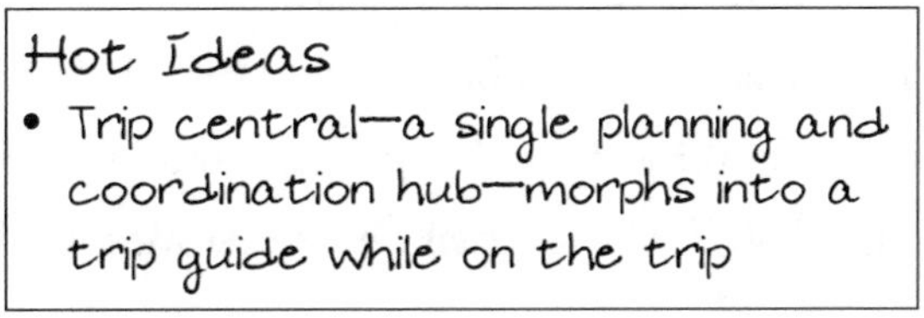

Figure 4.14: The beginnings of a hot ideas list captured from the team after walking the wall.

After walking the Affinity the facilitator introduces each of the Contextual Design models and participants read them in turn, individually or in pairs. They think about the implications of the data and post design ideas responding to it. Because each model presents a different aspect of the users' practice it prompts a different way of thinking about solutions for the design. The Identity model, for example, makes the users' self-image explicit and invites designers to think about how product features and overall product design can promote or violate the users' sense of self. The Day in the Life model promotes thinking about how an activity flows through place, time, and technology devices—a very different set of issues. After walking each set of models, the team adds to their lists of issues and hot ideas.

The Wall Walk provides an opportunity for individuals to dialog with the data and form an initial design response, getting ready for the visioning session. This interactive process focuses team members on how their design ideas respond to the user's world. Walking the data in a facilitated group process creates a time-bound, interactive event producing a tangible result focused on creating new product concepts.

The design ideas the team posts on the Affinity and on models are uncommitted, spur-of-the-moment ideas; Contextual Design does not encourage the team to get overly attached to them. But much of creativity comes through the recombination of existing parts. These ideas will be available to the team for reuse during the Visioning Session. Capturing the most systemic ideas in a list is an easy way for the team to share first ideas without committing to building anything—and without having to argue about whose idea is best. The bridge to design has to work not just for individual designers, but to bring the whole team together in a shared direction, without overly constraining design thinking or converging on a single solution too quickly. The Contextual Design ideation workshops are structured to do just that.

The Wall Walk is an immersion experience that can be used over and over with different teams for different purposes. Most complex products comprise multiple teams working on different parts; explicit consolidated data allows the different teams to walk the data and vision solutions for their own part of the problem. Because every team is responding to the same data, they are more likely to deliver a coherent response.

The Visioning Session. The Contextual Design Visioning Session is a facilitated workshop that generates a coherent design response to the user data. It is carefully structured to optimize a team's ability to invent creatively in the context of user data. It is a group process where the team jointly tells the story of the users' life and work, focusing on the tasks of interest, showing how the users' world will be changed and enhanced by the new invention. In the session, the team does multiple visions, telling multiple stories from different starting points, evaluates the visions, and then reconciles them to create a set of coherent product concepts. Here again, Contextual Design builds on people's natural skill at storytelling, using it now to generate new product ideas.

Structuring visioning as storytelling focuses the team on the coherent life of the user: because they are telling the story of the user's new life, the team has to make that life hang together. It has to make sense—the motivations and intentions envisioned for the user have to be realistic. Events, issues, and situations from the actual data can be folded into the story so the team can explore how the new design would resolve real situations in the users' lives. Because the team is thinking about how the life hangs together, the design will be holistic and coherent.

This structure for visioning also supports design in teams. Creative design requires a balance between *divergent* and *convergent* thinking—between coming up with multiple, disparate possibilities and settling on a single, mutually acceptable approach. Teams can limit creativity by converging too quickly on a single option without properly considering alternatives. This is what people are worrying about when they criticize "groupthink." The visioning process supports divergent thinking by allowing designers to each have their own, individual design ideas during the Wall Walk, and then leads the team to work out multiple possibilities in multiple visions. Then the process works towards convergence through the storytelling in the visions and by bringing the visions together into one high-level design.

Invention also requires putting off evaluation. It is not possible to be creative and evaluative at the same time—creativity requires free exploration, without worrying at every instant about whether an idea is practical or sounds silly. The Visioning Session puts off evaluation until after all the stories are told so that the visions themselves can be free of the "yes buts..." that get in the way of the flow of creative thought.

Finally, detail is the enemy of creativity—but engineers love detail. If a team stops and works out the details of every idea as soon as they have it, they'll move very slowly, and won't be very creative. In fact, speed is the friend of creativity. It allows designers to move quickly enough over the whole design to keep all the parts together, without getting stuck on one part. The visioning process keeps the team operating at a high level, moving down to successively more detail in later steps.

Creating a vision: A vision starts with a hot idea off the list made earlier. Based on that idea, the team starts storytelling. One person starts describing what a user—usually one of the personas—will do in the new world, inventing product features as they go. Others share their ideas as the story develops, so it becomes a team creation. As they talk, one person plays the role of *pen* and draws the ideas on a flip chart as a coherent, pictorial story.

Team members see their vision becoming concrete on a flip chart as they talk and are encouraged to build on each other's contributions to generate the story. No one criticizes another's contribution—if they see an issue with an idea, they think about how to fix it and propose a solution. The storytelling continues until the team runs out of ideas or until the scenario reaches a natural end. Because the discussion gets lively, it's best to restrict a visioning team to no more than eight people—several teams can vision in parallel if you want more people to be involved. A vision should take 20–40 minutes to create, depending on the complexity of the practice being supported.

When the team decides a vision is complete enough, they put it aside, turn to another hot idea, and do another vision. Because each vision is, by design, systemic and holistic, it is quite likely that a vision incorporates more than one hot idea. So after each vision, the team re-evaluates which hot ideas have been covered and which will be most interesting to do next. It is rarely necessary to do a separate vision for every hot idea. Similarly, because the people in the vision session walked the wall, they already have their design ideas in their heads—as the story of the user's new world emerges they naturally pull in their own ideas, adjusting them to the story that's being told.

A team typically completes 4-6 visions to address a design problem. In some areas the visions are likely to build on each other—"We'll just handle that the way we did in the last vision," the team might say. In other areas, the visions will be independent. In others, they will be incompatible. This is expected.

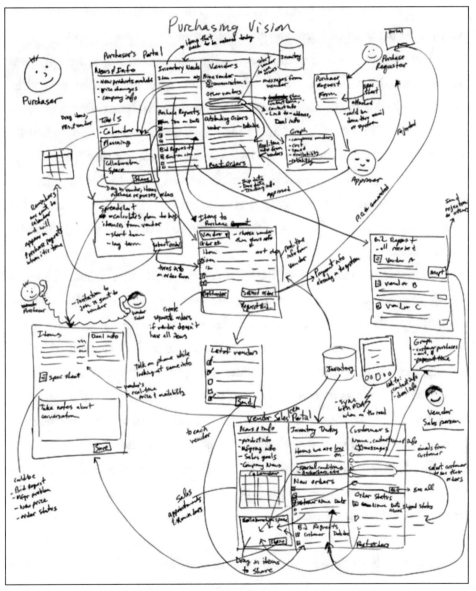

Figure 4.15: A vision created by a team—hand-drawn, on a flip chart. Ability to draw is not a necessary skill for the pen.

Vision evaluation: Once the team completes visioning they can bring their evaluative thinking to bear on the emerging design ideas as a separate step. This is itself a design step—identifying aspects of a vision that don't work prompts the team to generate new design solutions that work better. On the flip side, identifying what is working makes good ideas explicit, ensuring they are not lost and that everyone on the team understands why they matter.

The critique in vision evaluation is tightly structured. There are only three valid issues with a vision: lack of fit to user practice, technical difficulty, and incompatibility with the business mission. In evaluation, the team first lists all the aspects of the vision that work (they fit user practice, are easy to do technically, or fit the business mission), then the issues and problems. As they list problems, they are encouraged to suggest design ideas to address them. In this way, the team implicitly prioritizes what they want to take forward and what they want to let go from their initial design thinking without having to have a heavyweight prioritization process.

Identifying product concepts: The vision stories imply new product concepts. Any significant product is composed of feature sets, app suites, and related services that work together. The visions contain these concepts within a story of to-be use. But they will be developed and delivered as coherent product elements that have to hang together coherently. Each product concept holds together and could (in theory) be delivered as its own product. If the team's only view of their design is as a set of scenarios, they will only see the features—they will not see how the concepts have their own structure, relationships, and coherence.

The final step of the Visioning Session is to identify the product concepts explicitly. Each vision suggests product concepts that may have been built up across other visions. The vision evaluation makes it easier to identify the coherent product concepts because the evaluation focuses on the vision elements, not the entire scenario. For example, in our travel project the team identified a research tool, with a collection area for ideas and an app for in-the-moment research; a planning tool for laying out the trip and making sure all logistics have been considered; and an app for taking on the trip to record and share memorable events.

These product concepts work together as a whole solution, but each can be thought about and refined on its own.

The team draws each product concept separately, pulling the best ideas for that concept from all the visions, using the design ideas and vision elements from one vision to solve problems identified in another. This process encourages the team to think of each vision not as a monolithic whole, but as a grab-bag of parts that can be recombined and repurposed to both solve the users' problem and bring value to the business organization. These high-level product concepts feed the next phase of ideation. This is also a good time to share the vision with management stakeholders to check direction.

4.3.2   THE COOL DRILLDOWN

The final part of high level ideation is the *Cool Drilldown* workshop. Design for life means designing to fit the whole life, including structure of activities throughout the time and places of the day, motivations, attitude, and self-image. Designers are not used to addressing these aspects of design, so it is easy to overlook them in the visioning session. Getting these aspects of design right also requires more detailed design than the quick construction of visions allows for. The visioning session is intentionally fast-paced. There's no time to engage in a reflective conversation exploring the implications of each Cool Concept—and with at least a rough idea of product direction such reflection is more worthwhile. So once the Visioning Session has produced a set of clear product concepts the team can take time to consider how to design in a cool user experience.

The Cool Drilldown guides designers through the implications of each Cool Concept and its associated principles for their design. Each Cool Concept focuses on a different aspect of life and implies different design principles—what should be designed in to best produce a transformative experience. No one person or team can reasonably consider all these dimensions simultaneously without getting overwhelmed and losing focus. So the Cool Drilldown workshop focuses the team

---

Identifying product concepts in this way also supports iterative development processes. It would be natural to assign each product concept to a different Scrum team, for example; and the vision elements can be quickly evolved into user stories.

on one new product concept and one Cool Concept at a time. The team works in small groups in parallel, so they can move very quickly. Designers become more aware of the design principles for cool and produce enriched product concepts in a reasonable length of time.

In the Cool Drilldown workshop, the team starts by identifying the product concepts they want to cover, usually about 4–6 concepts. Taking each product concept in turn, they break into sub-teams. Each sub-team focuses on a different Cool Concept. Using the 8–10 design principles associated with each concept, individual sub-teams optimize the same product concept according to the design principles associated with their Cool Concept. They use the data on the Affinity and Contextual Design models to feed their more detailed thinking with the actual customer data; then they brainstorm and sketch additions to the product concept that will enhance the cool user experience based on principles for their Cool Concept. This focused design process is another way of bridging from data to design, using design principles important for creating a transformative user experience.

Each subteam does this same drilldown on a different Cool Concept in parallel. In this way a single product concept is simultaneously enhanced to get the flow of life done better (Accomplishment), make connections to people that matter easier (Connection), support identity elements explicitly (Identity), create delightful and useful graphics and animation (Sensation), provide more direct interaction (Direct/Hassle), and eliminate learning as a task (Learning Delta). But now each subteam has developed ideas independently, so the product concept is no longer coherent. So after the subteams do their work, all these independent enhancements to the product concept are brought back together in a full team review session and reconciled into a single, revised design concept incorporating the best parts of all drilldowns. The result is a product design that addresses more of the Cool Concepts and addresses them better, and therefore is more effective and desirable.

Each product concept is addressed in this way, resulting in a richer set of high-level designs. Subteams shift from one Cool Concept to another as they optimize different product concepts so they get familiar with all of them. In this way, they learn how to design for cool without getting overwhelmed. At the end of the workshop the team has internalized the customer data, has experience working with the cool principles, and has a shared understanding of what they would like to build in the future.

Now, with a sound conceptual design in hand, the team is poised to develop real function and a designed UI. That is the province of the third part of Contextual Design.

CHAPTER 5

Detailed Design and Validation

The third part of Contextual Design deals with design itself: to take the concept developed in Visioning Session and elaborated in the Cool Drilldown and give it a structure, function, interaction, and look that enhances the users' lives. Creating good, innovative designs has always been hard; now that connected devices are everywhere, fitting into life at every moment, the design task has only gotten harder and getting it right more critical. At the same time, Agile processes [5, 6] have reduced the time available for focused design thinking. The steps in this third part of Contextual Design are designed to thread this needle—just enough focused thinking to create a coherent design combined with quick and early prototyping and iteration to refine the work in progress.

Designing all the parts of a product so they work together coherently is hard. It was always hard, even with large monolithic systems like standard ERP systems and big websites, and it's even harder when designers have to create apps that fit into moments in the person's day. It's easy to get lost in the weeds, focusing on one part of one app, and lose any sense of the overall structure and its relationship to people's lives. The challenge is to keep that structure in mind and ensure its coherence even while working on the details of one part. Designers need tools that represent the overall structure so they can analyze and discuss it independent of the details of any part. (This is why web designers create site maps—they are a structural view of the site that show all the parts and their relationships at a high level.) Below, we'll share Contextual Design techniques and team-based activities that help the team see their design structurally at every point—and so ensure the whole team shares the same understanding of the emerging design.

In describing the design process it's convenient to think of design in layers, starting with an abstract and fuzzy concept and refining it to produce a specific UI with precisely defined function and interaction. We will describe Contextual

Design's steps this way. But remember in the sections that follow, that these layers are not addressed purely sequentially, one after another, as if this were a waterfall model. That doesn't work. Not only would it require a long design phase—anathema to Agile development—but the layers inform each other. If designers know that infinite scrolling (a low-level interaction paradigm) is available, it will change how they think about higher layers of the design. So in each iteration each layer of design is touched lightly to produce a provisional design for the product. User feedback usually addresses all layers at once, because users see the product holistically. But when designers can see and think structurally they can focus early feedback on validating the structure and product concept, saving UI details for later iterations when the structure is stable.

In Contextual Design, the design phase comprises three primary layers. The first is *practice design*: figuring out how the user moves through the system in the course of their activity (even if it is spread out over time, place, and device), with the right function and information available at every point. It's where the life of the user meets the functionality and structure of the product. Practice design defines virtual "places" that support the different parts of the overall activity cleanly: everything necessary and nothing extra. Practice design includes the behavior of the system, including adaptive algorithms such as learning the user's preferences by example. Practice design does not worry about how places and functions show up visually—that's a concern for the lower layers of design (remembering always that layers are not cleanly separated in time).

Practice design uses scenarios, use cases, and user stories to explore the different tasks, activities, and situations the user may encounter and how the product will support them. When your user data shows that people have to go to 87 separate places to do their job (a real example, from the insurance industry), you know already that your system has problems. Contextual Design uses storyboards to ensure that the scenarios of use are coherent. Storyboards make the team think through the practice coherently, ensuring the user experience makes sense.

Practice design is where true, game-changing innovation happens. This is where the new product concepts from ideation are made real. Innovation at lower layers of design can improve the product, but doesn't introduce fundamental improvements in how activities are done or the important goals of life are supported. That kind of transformation of life has to happen here; support of the Wheel of Joy in Life happens here. We emphasize this because this is also the easiest layer to skip—it's seductive to jump right into sketching out UIs and designing pages. You can even get away with it, in that you'll still have a product at the end. But you won't have the innovation you might have had if you had looked at practice redesign first.

The next layer we identify in Contextual Design is *interaction design*. It's an overused term, but useful: by it we mean designing the layout of the screens and the users' basic interaction with them, independent of the specific graphical look. Interaction design might specify a top navigation bar for a specific purpose, and an area to display the primary content. It might specify infinite scrolling, expand-in-place, and swipe-sideways for the content area. It would not specify font, color, or graphical decoration on any of those parts. Good interaction design ensures that each place defined in practice design has a layout that clearly presents the purpose and function available in that place—even a good design can be destroyed by interaction design that obscures the purpose of the place. Creating a real Direct into Action user experience happens here; a central concern at this layer is to support the concepts in the Triangle of Joy in Use.

There are two structural elements for designers to focus on during interaction design. The first is the structure of the screen itself, independent of specific elements on that screen. A clean screen structure is easy for the user to make sense of. The second is the consistency of screen structure across the design, so that as the user moves from screen to screen—and device to device—the basic structure is consistent, familiar, and comfortable.

Interaction design also covers the design of the content being presented. Access to information—content—is a critical part of many products supporting connected lives. How content can be found and scanned, how different content elements relate to each other, the tone in which it is written—these are complex issues (check Amazon to appreciate how complex) and need to be designed explicitly.

The final layer we define is the *visual design*, in which the graphical treatment, colors, branding, animation, and details of interaction are defined. Visual design structures the users' experience by what it emphases, how it uses graphical elements and white space to draw the eye and lead it through the page, and how it uses interactions to guide the user. (An example of the last is the "bounce" introduced by the iPhone to show that the user has reached the end of a scrolling list.) Well done, the visual design reinforces and emphasizes the purpose and structure designed by higher layers of the design process.

Visual design has its own structural aspect. It has to ensure consistency of look and experience across the whole product, regardless of platform. This is where the Sensation Model helps the designer determine what tone, brand, feel they want to communicate. Aesthetic design contributes to the cool user experience of any product. But as we found in the Cool Concept of Sensation, people expect a modern, well-done visual design; delivering anything less reduces the experience of cool. Gratuitous animation, abrasive sounds, or unappealing color undermines that experience. Getting the visual design right matters and enhances products—*if* good practice and interaction design are already in place.

So design is a layered activity, with a natural sequence to the layers, each layer having its own concerns and its own issues and requiring somewhat different expertise. Visual designers need to understand graphics and color; UX designers need to understand how users approach systems. Yet the layers are also interdependent, and in an iterative process design at the different layers proceeds in parallel. Managing this design conversation is hard. It's easy to get lost in the layers—if a designer objects to a button, are they objecting to the button itself, its look? Or are they objecting to the function the button represents? Or merely its place on the page? When different roles, such as user researcher, interaction designer, and visual designer, with different skills and language, are all on the team together the conversation gets even more complex. Contextual Design helps a team separate the conversations—even when they're happening at the same time—so that everyone knows what is being discussed.

The layers of design overlap not only because they inform each other, but because the design is created iteratively. Iteration with user feedback is fundamental to this phase of Contextual Design. It keeps the design on track. Designers sitting in a room talking to each other—even when they start from user data—get lost in the details of a design. They think too hard about points that don't matter and argue too long about questions that can only be resolved by the user. They spend vast amounts of time developing a feature only to discover, on user test, that users don't value that feature—and then they're too invested in it to give it up easily. So Contextual Design encourages a quick trip through the layers of design, taking the result out to users for feedback, and using that feedback to redirect the design.* The first iteration may be very rough, and that's fine. Later iterations will refine the design, add detail, and finally result in a polished product.

There's also a good business reason for early prototyping and iteration. Putting your concept in front of users gives you early feedback on whether the concept itself is any good, and helps you make the business case for developing the product. Field interviews can validate the basic concept while getting feedback on the presentation layer. And if the Cool Metric is used at the same time, feedback from the score can tell the team what dimensions of the cool user experience are strong or weak. Together, the user feedback and score can guide the team in design changes. If the Cool Metric was used on a prior product or competitive product, the team can compare their scores to the other product to make sure they are moving in the right direction.

The result of explicitly designing in layers is a flexible process that works well with modern iterative development practices, such as Agile and Lean UX [7]. We'll now walk through the activities of Contextual Design for detailed design: Interaction Design Patterns, Storyboarding, User Environment Design, and

---

* This is a similar approach to that advocated by Lean Design—get quickly to a prototype good enough to test your key design questions and no more. When those questions are answered, then you're ready for the next level of detail.

Validation testing. We will discuss each in turn, but remember throughout that in practice they happen in parallel and continuously interact with each other.

5.1   INTERACTION DESIGN PATTERNS

To ensure that the team has the best modern design materials, they start by looking at existing *interaction design patterns* for inspiration. Once possible high-level approaches are identified, the interaction design patterns evolve and are iterated along with the other aspects of the product's overall design.

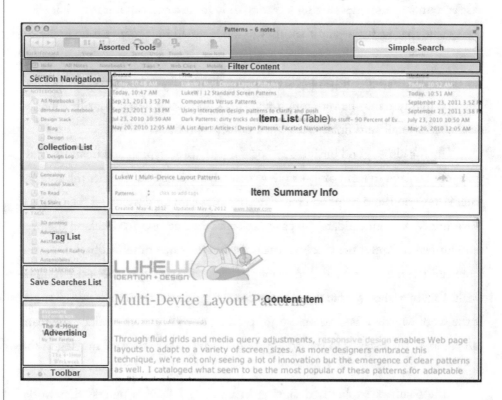

Figure 5.1: An interaction pattern analysis of a website showing the primary components of the screen.

Interaction design patterns define how function might be presented, the structure of the pages, access to content on the pages, and navigation across pages. These interaction design patterns give the team a way to think structurally about the design they are creating without getting caught up in lower-level and graphical details. This step ensures that the design team stops to think about what constitutes a modern design and what techniques and trends of interaction design are important to their situation. Seeing how others have approached designs similar to their own product concept widens the team's vision of what is possible—especially when they look to other domains and types of products. It enhances the team's knowledge of interaction design materials. This is not mere copying: this analysis jump-starts the designers' own creativity by giving them a set of options and a starting point. And since most designers are visual thinkers, having such a visual representation is an important aid to creativity.

To generate these preliminary interaction design patterns, the team starts with the sketches of the product concepts from the Cool Drilldown. While these sketches will not define all function and every page, the central areas and most important function to be designed will be represented. These are the places and interactions the team has to think about and define interaction patters for.

The team then explores how other products have approached similar problems. They deliberately choose sites and products that will challenge their entering assumptions about how such an interface should be structured. Business applications can benefit from looking at consumer products for hints on creating modern interfaces.

For modern interface design, materials include design elements such as carousels that show lots of information in a small space, responsive nav bars that orient the user as well as showing available options, buttons that appear and overlay content only when needed, and teaser content that expands in place to show a full article, to name just a few. Such interaction elements have come to be expected by users and must be at the designers' fingertips so that they can be incorporated into a design. But interaction design technologies and industry trends advance and change. Continuously re-familiarizing a team with modern design practices is the best way to ensure they are designing with the latest materials. Then the team can recombine and change mechanisms from sites they analyze, adding new elements, to come up with their own preliminary interaction design structure.

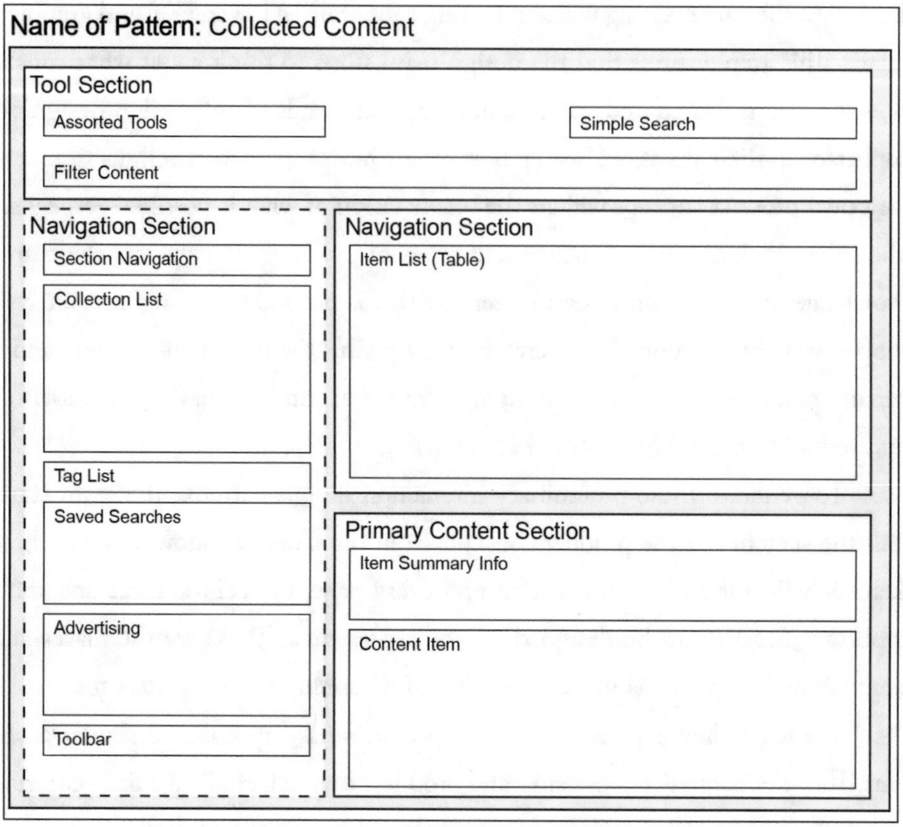

Name of Pattern: Collected Content

Tool Section
Assorted Tools
Simple Search
Filter Content

Navigation Section
Section Navigation
Collection List
Tag List
Saved Searches
Advertising
Toolbar

Navigation Section
Item List (Table)

Primary Content Section
Item Summary Info
Content Item

Figure 5.2: An interaction design pattern for collecting content across the Web, showing the primary screen areas that support the overall task. The level of detail in this pattern is typical of one created prior to UI design; prior to storyboarding there may be less detail.

The team creates an interaction design pattern for each major screen in the design, as identified in the Cool Drilldown. They use ideas from the comparative sites as appropriate, thereby building on users' expectations in this domain, but modify and revise as needed for their own design problem. The interaction patterns depend on the platform (phone, tablet, desktop), in which case a pattern is created for each platform. The team also has to have a concept of how pages might work on a touch vs. computer interface—and if interactions such as disclosure of hidden content will operate by different mechanisms on different devices. Each platform has its own interaction standards to take into consideration and steal from. It is never too early to get the team to think cross-platform so that they will take that breadth of thinking into storyboarding.

The interaction design patterns act as a framework for designers, focusing them on the structure of the page and the structure of the system from a UI perspective. The patterns focus the team on thinking structurally about the user interface, which moves them away from thinking only about functions or look of the page. Pushing the team to think structurally ensures greater consistency within and across the system. And by starting the team with these initial interaction patterns the team simultaneously uses modern design approaches and principles while they are reinventing the practice.

As we said above, the layers inform each other. Creating these initial interaction patterns helps designers imagine a user interacting with them, using functions suggested by the patterns, as they follow the scenarios fleshed out in storyboarding. These interaction patterns will change as the team works through the low-level design, but they provide a concrete starting point. They introduce less experienced teams to design possibilities already out in the world which they can use as-is or revise for their own purposes. Experienced teams use them to think about what they will add to push the envelope, guided by the Cool Design principles.

5.2   STORYBOARDING

Storyboards help the team work out how specific user activities and situations will be handled by the new design. They sketch the sequence of events as a story, drawing each step to show users, screens, and their interactions on each platform. A storyboard ensures that the work and life of the user are supported by the new product. Storyboards work through different cases, tasks, and situations to define how the new design will support them. They work much like storyboards for a movie, which show what happens in each scene without going into too much detail about any scene. It's easy to break the users' existing practice by jumping from the big new idea to low-level user interface and implementation design without con-sidering the impact it has on the flow of the user's activities. As soon as designers start focusing on technology, technology and its problems become their central design concern. Storyboards work against this tendency.

Storyboards also limit the level of detail at this point in the design process. A storyboard cell can only hold so much; a drawing of a UI within a cell can only describe so much detail. The preliminary interaction patterns suggest structure and function without pushing the team into too much detail. All this helps keep designers from diving down into the small details of their design before the overall product structure has been settled. Especially when a design addresses multiple platforms, the team needs to see the overall coherence of the activity as it moves across time, place, and platform before being caught up in the many details of each platform's UI.

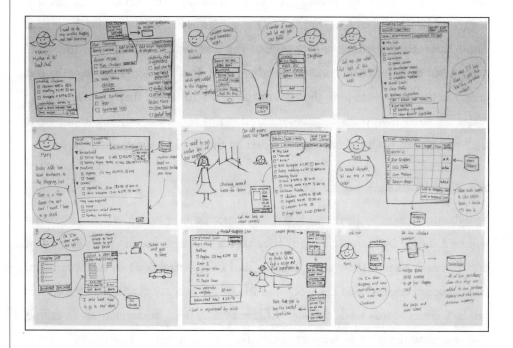

Figure 5.3: A storyboard working out the steps of one interaction with the system. The story is fed by the consolidated Sequence models and by the vision. Elements of the screens drawn in storyboard cells are suggested by the initial interaction design patterns.

Storyboards encourage the team to use story thinking, designing the whole flow of life to show how the user will move through time and place to get their activities done. Then, when they have finished the primary scenarios of use, they can look across their storyboards and optimize how the system hangs together as a product offering. Only then do they worry about how to structure the product appropriately for each platform. Optimizing an interface for one scenario will not yield an optimized system or suite of apps, so it's essential to get the practice right before settling on any system or UI structure.

The process of storyboarding keeps the team honest and the design clean. Guided by the affinity diagram and consolidated models, the product concepts are made real in these stories. Storyboards ensure that the team does not overlook any intents or steps that are critical to the users' practice. Even when the design changes the practice, designers have to think through the details of how it will be changed to ensure that the new approach works and adoption is easy. The consolidated field data and Contextual Design models help focus the team on the world they are designing for so they can get real about what they are doing to the user.

Storyboards flesh out the product concepts by grounding them in the stories and motives of users' lives. They are guided by the consolidated models, which describe how users have different identities, relationships, patterns of life, and collaboration styles—all of which need to be accounted for in the storyboards. If different users approach a task different ways, a storyboard is created for each different way to show how the new product will work in that situation. The team uses the storyboards to invent the right function and the right product structure to support each user situation.

Separate storyboards are created for each main task and each main user situation. A team might start with a "happy path" storyboard showing the user doing the task in the simple case where everything works, designing places and functions as they are needed. They follow the Day-In-Life model scenario showing the how the product will support the activity when the work starts at home, is interrupted, continues during the user's commute on their mobile device, and is finished during a break at work—reflecting how people use devices now. They draw storyboard cells showing manual steps, rough user interface components, movement through the world, app and device use, and system activity and automation.

But then the team needs to create a range of storyboards to explore the dif-ferent issues important to this particular design. So after the "happy path" case, they do variants showing different problems and difficult user situations found in the data. The team uses storyboards to explore design for different platforms: how the activities of the task to be supported will be accessed through different plat-forms, what to provide on each platform, and how to keep the activity coherent across devices. The team designs for time, how useful things will get done in mo-ments, and for relationships, supporting meaningful connection in the context of the activity at hand. Overall, the team generates the key scenarios they must walk through to have a complete design—all guided by the user data.

After each task has been thought through and sketched, the team reviews it to ensure that it remains true to the customer data and the Cool Concepts. This ensures that the design accounts for the users' strategies, tasks, and issues and that new inventions either support the users' practice or give them a better way to approach it. A design might change all the existing steps of an activity and even eliminate whole activities altogether; as long as people can still achieve their fundamental intents, the change will work. When teams forget or ignore the user's intent, the design is in trouble.

Design with storyboards ensures the design accounts for the context of use. But the context is not just the task being supported, or how features are structured and grouped in a product; the context that matters is the overall life of the user and the way any activity fits into that life. Storyboarding brings this context into focus for the team during the detailed design process.

5.3   THE USER ENVIRONMENT DESIGN

Storyboards explore how a design supports the flow of the user's life. But there is another, equally important aspect of design, which is the *structure of the system*: laying out the parts of the product so they make sense as a system. Design alter-nates between these two perspectives, first telling stories about a new system, story thinking, then organizing the parts of the system structurally to see what they imply, which is structural thinking. Contextual Design provides the User Environment Design (UED) to show basic structure and function (Figure 26). The UED can be used to design a new product, show additions to an existing product, or represent a suite of apps and products that share data in a mobile world. Just as architects draw floor plans to see the structure and flow of a house, the UED shows designers the virtual floor plan of their new system.

The UED shows the structure of a product as a set of *focus areas*, places within the system that provide support for coherent activities. A focus area might be a window, web page, or screen. The UED shows each part of the system—how it supports the user's activities, exactly what function is available in that part, how it is organized in an interaction design pattern, and how the user gets to and from other parts of the system. When complete, the UED breaks the function and content of the system into coherent places that work to support all the scenarios of use.

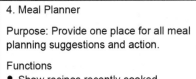 

Figure 5.4: A single focus area (left) and interaction design pattern (right). The focus area defines what happens in the place; the design pattern provides the basic layout for presentation of the place.

Each focus area in the final UED is associated with an interaction design pattern to be used to present the function. The organization of content and function within a focus area is another aspect of structural design: *the structure of the interface*. Structural design of the interface looks at the organization of the focus areas and communication between them, the layout of each focus area's interface, and how a person interacts with it.

If a design supports multiple devices, focus areas in the UED may be specific to a device. The UED needs to show how an activity flows across devices, supported by the system. This is best done by showing interfaces on different devices as separate focus areas, even when the function overlaps significantly. The interaction design patterns associated with each focus area allow the team to scan across the system and ensure that the interaction is consistent everywhere. It's best to print out the focus areas and spread them out on a table or wall—this allows the designers to scan across the whole system easily. Then they can redesign and tune the system structure and interaction design patterns used across the system for optimal use both in each focus area and across the system. It allows developers to look at the functions of each focus areas to be sure they can deliver the function, automation, and data needed to support that place.

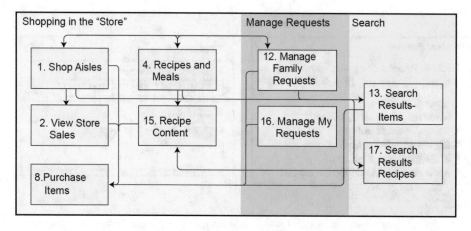

Figure 5.5: A UED for an online grocery shopping system. This UED map shows just the focus areas and connections between them supporting flow through the system.

To create a UED, the team walks the storyboards and pulls out the implications of what the system needs to do to support each cell, defining focus areas and functions as they go. As the implications of storyboard after storyboard are rolled into the UED, the team starts to see the best way to structure the system—

whether delivered on the Web or on the desktop, as a set mobile apps or one monolithic system. When storyboards show activities crossing different platforms, the UED reveals how each platform may share structure and function with other platforms or may provide unique variants suitable to that platform.

Documenting the product design with the UED provides a roadmap that can later—after validation—be used to create Agile releases, user stories, prioritize roll out over multiple product versions, or hand off to different groups to work in parallel.

5.4   TESTING AND ITERATION

At this point, the team is ready to complete the interaction design knowing that the structure of the system makes sense. But it's important to recognize that neither the structure, nor the UI, nor even the product concept has been validated with users. Is this product concept something anyone wants to buy or use? Will this structure actually work in the context of users' real lives? An iterative approach to design says a team should do the minimum work necessary to create a prototype just good enough to give reliable feedback on whether the basic design concepts work. A complete design is not necessary to start this validation process—you don't need a fully rendered visual treatment or even all parts of the system fully defined.

Contextual Design focuses on how to validate and iterate product designs to ensure that teams build the right thing for their users and their business. So we will skip over the details of how to design a good UI—there are lots of other good books on these disciplines that we don't need to duplicate. Our emphasis is on using structural thinking in the UED and interaction design patterns to get the basics right, then doing quick iterations with users to refine the details and nail down latent needs.

In Contextual Design testing and iteration starts by creating a rough prototype of the design, usually in paper, and having users work with the prototype in field interviews. Users cannot give good feedback if presented with models or even storyboards directly—such design artifacts are too abstract, and too much of users' knowledge of their own work is tacit. However, users can interact with a user interface mockup and talk about their reactions. If the product is a device, they can hold it in their hands and experience the form factor. So to test ideas, a team moves quickly through initial storyboarding, UED, and UI design, and produces a rough user interface as soon as possible. This rough user interface is mocked up and tested with users. Typically, the time from ideation to mockup interview is only a few weeks.

Mockup interviews help designers understand why design elements work or fail and help to identify needed new function, especially latent needs that could not be discovered until the user started interacting with the design. This iterative testing starts with rough mockups built using ordinary stationery supplies (Figure 5.6). Rough prototypes provide several advantages: they are quick to build; they communicate to the user that the design is incomplete and invite feedback; they are easy to modify during the prototype interview to instantly try out changes and new design ideas; and they focus users and designers on the fundamental structure, high-level interaction pattern, and top function of the prototype, rather than low-level details of the user interface. And they can quickly represent the product function across multiple platforms.

The prototype is built so that it tests the most important issues of the design. (Lean UX embodies the same philosophy: identify and test critical points early.) If the design is to work on mobile devices, the prototype may be implemented as smartphone-sized cards to test whether it can be useful in that size and in real life contexts. We test such designs with people while they are on the go, not just in their homes or offices. If the product collects and presents information, as many task support systems do, real content is developed and embedded in the prototype so that users can experience having such content available at the moment of need. This helps us test content tone, length, clarity, and structure.

A mockup interview is based on the principles of Contextual Inquiry described earlier: We test with users in their *contexts* to keep them grounded in their real practices. Users interact with the prototype by playing out their own activities within the mock-up manipulating and modifying the prototype directly. The *part-*

nership is one of co-design: as the user works with the prototype, performing a task they need to do or did in the recent past, the user and designer uncover what works and delights—and they uncover problems and adjust the prototype to fix them. Together the user and interviewer *interpret* what is going on in the usage and come up with alternative designs. The overall *focus* of the interview is to understand what works and what doesn't in the prototype—and whether there is perceived value.

The team may decide to administer the Cool Metric as part of evaluating how they are doing during each round of iteration. The Cool Metric is presented at the end of the interview, after the user has experienced the product idea and so can give a meaningful score. This measurement tool allows the team to get a quick read on their new design—how well are they supporting the Cool Concepts? How much of an improvement is it? And where is it weak so there are opportunities for improvement? The score points to strengths and weaknesses to be addressed in the next round of redesign.

The context of the interview is designed to mimic as closely as possible the context of real use. For example, when making new interfaces for automobiles, one team put mockups on the dashboard of the users' own car and played pre-recorded audio from an iPod and mini speaker. In the test, they drove with users in their cars, imitating the verbal and visual messages of the new system. In this way the design team saw the user's actual response in their car while driving. They discussed the user's reaction with them and, co-designing, determined the best way to communicate to a driver. In the same way, mockups for mobile devices can be presented as cards on the target device itself, so designers can see how the device affects user interaction.

After the design has been tested with four to six users (depending on the scope of the project), the team redesigns to reflect the feedback. The Cool Metric score (if used) and design principles from the Cool Concepts inform the redesign. Multiple rounds of mockup interviews and iteration allow design and testing in increasing levels of detail. Over the course of the rounds of mockup interviews the team moves from rough representations to wireframes with increasing detail, to on-line clickable prototypes—possibly with a visual design treatment so that can be tested as well.

Prototypes get more and more realistic as structure, layout, and user value are established. When prototyping for mobile devices or for product concepts that cross platforms we need to test on all platforms and situations to see how the flow from platform to platform works. For low-level user interaction, especially for touch interfaces, a working prototype that runs on the target platform may be essential to really see what is happening in those momentary interactions. But it is still best for the initial prototypes to be in paper because they encourage change—they invite the user into the conversation about overall product value, high level function, base interaction paradigm, and other elements of core structure.

After two rounds of testing (with a redesign pass after each round to address the issues found in each round), it is helpful to do a Cool Drilldown review of the design. As with storyboards and with visioning, doing the work of test and redesign requires the team to focus on the many details of the design. It is inevitable that they will get lost in the details. A review process at this point reinforces a structural view—it rebuilds their sense of the overall product and user interface structure and gives the team perspective on whether they could address the Cool Concepts better. This shift in perspective forces them out of the weeds and gives them a framework for coming to the design afresh. Revisions to the design from this Cool Drilldown can be folded into the next round of mockup interviews.

We find that three rounds of testing are generally enough. After three rounds, the team has finalized the structure of the product, the basic interaction design, the content type and tone, any navigation structure or information architecture, and has clarified any business rules. The third round usually starts testing detailed user interface and interaction paradigms that are hard to test in paper, so it may need to be online. The third round can also include a preliminary visual design. These interviews may be remote—after two rounds of face-to-face testing in paper, a third round of remote interviews can work well. Finally, a highly interactive design may benefit from a fourth round to ensure the visual design and touch interactions really work.

In an Agile process the third round of design may overlap with the first round of development—the online prototype may in fact be the first iteration of development work. From that point forward the UX designers and coders should work in a tight partnership, with the developers passing working code to UX designers and UX designers passing feedback and new designs to developers [8].

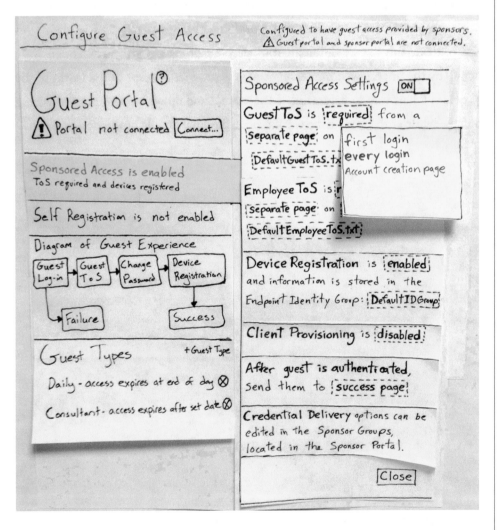

Figure 5.6: A sample paper prototype. Parts of the UI are differentiated with sticky notes; information is hand-written so it can be added to or changed with users on the fly. Note that the popup leaves space for adding or changing information in the moment.

The validation rounds of prototype interviews take the product concepts back into the real world of the user and put them in the context of the user's life. This is another round of immersion and "get real" for the design team. It is the ultimate test of product reception—inviting the user to do their real tasks using a mockup in a "let's pretend" situation instead of getting a demo and being asked for an opinion. Just as in the initial Contextual Inquiry interviews, people can respond with reliable information when they are doing their own activities in their own life context. This is very different from a lab or simulator with pre-defined tasks set up by the interviewer. Immersing the new product concept in the world of the user is the best way to determine if the team came up with something of lasting value—while at the same time working out the final details of the design itself.

CHAPTER 6

Conclusion

Contextual Design encourages holistic, systemic design, looking at the whole work and life context of use and responding with an integrated design that broadly supports user activities. From visioning through validation the team takes a large, loose product concept and turns it into a detailed design that can guide product specification and rollout planning. With customer data documented and at hand, and with the UED and UI specifications written down and tested with users, product managers and design teams can plan their development rollout using whatever methodology the company prefers. Contextual Design produces the product concepts needed for the next step of development, whether that is to write product requirement documents, functional specifications, Agile user stories, or something else. Contextual Design drives these concepts from a deep understanding of the users and supports the design team with design processes that keep that user focus front and center.

Good design has always been difficult. With the introduction of mobile devices, always on and always connected, design has only gotten more difficult and more exciting. The potential impact of a new product on human lives is more profound and more valuable than ever. But to do it right, teams need a design process that is sensitive to the larger world of the user, steeps them in that world, and guides them to use what they have learned to produce products that are successful. The context of use today is much richer and more complex than ever before; the impact on people's lives is much more profound, and the technological possibilities are much deeper and more wide-ranging.

In our industry, the design processes we use must grow to meet these new challenges. Whereas it used to be merely desirable to immerse designers in the users' context, a deep understanding of the users' lives is now critical to developing a successful product at all. Designers need not only a process for going into the field and finding out about users, but also a conceptual framework for making sense of what they discover. They need a way to use that data for the purpose of innovation and a set of design principles that will drive them to meet the challenges of modern product design

Contextual Design, augmented by the insights of The Cool Project, has met these new challenges with new concepts, models, and activities needed to develop a modern design. We hope that this discussion has provided some insight into what these new challenges are and how they may be successfully met by the processes our industry uses.

References

[1] Beyer, H. and Holtzblatt, K. *Contextual Design: Defining Customer-Centered Systems*, Morgan Kaufmann Publishers Inc., San Francisco, 1997.

[2] Holtzblatt, K., Wendell, J., and Wood, S. *Rapid Contextual Design: A How-to Guide to Key Techniques for User-Centered Design*, Morgan Kaufmann Publishers, San Francisco, CA, 2005. DOI: 10.1145/1066322.1066325.

[3] Holtzblatt, K. and Holtzblatt, S. "Communicating user research in order to drive design and product decisions," in *CHI '14 Extended Abstracts on Human Factors in Computing Systems (CHI EA '14)*, 2014. ACM, New York, NY, USA, 1155-1158. DOI: 10.1145/2559206.2559207.

[4] Cooper, A. *The Inmates Are Running the Asylum: Why High Tech Products Drive Us Crazy and How to Restore the Sanity*, Sams Publishing, Indiana, 1997.

[5] Beck, K. and Andres, C. *Extreme Programming Explained: Embrace Change*, 2nd ed., Addison-Wesley, 2005.

[6] Schwaber, K. and Sutherland, J. *Software in 30 Days: How Agile Managers Beat the Odds, Delight Their Customers, And Leave Competitors In the Dust*, John Wiley & Sons, 2012.

[7] Gothelf, J. and Seiden, J. *Lean UX: Applying Lean Principles to Improve User Experience*. O'Reilly Media, Incorporated, 2013.

[8] Beyer, H. *User-Centered Agile Methods*, Morgan & Claypool Publishers, 2010. DOI: 10.2200/S00286ED1V01Y201002HCI010.

Author Biographies

Karen Holtzblatt, CEO and Co-founder of InContext, is the visionary behind InContext's unique customer-centered design approach, Contextual Design. Karen's combination of technological and psychological expertise provides the creative framework for driving the development, innovative designs, and design processes.

Recognized as a leader in requirements and design, Karen has pioneered transformative ideas and design approaches throughout her career. Most recently, Karen initiated the Cool Project to explore users' experience of cool products. The November issue of *Interactions* showcases the core factors affecting the "cool" user experience in the cover story, "What Makes Things Cool?" http://see.sc/x5v1cz3os.

Karen introduced Contextual Inquiry, now the industry standard for gathering field data to understand how technology impacts the way people work. Contextual Inquiry and the design processes based on it provide a revolutionary approach for designing new products and systems based on a deep understanding of the context of use. Contextual Inquiry forms the base of Contextual Design, InContext's full customer-centered design process.

Karen co-founded InContext Design in 1992 to use Contextual Design techniques to coach product teams and deliver market data and design solutions to businesses across multiple industries. The books, *Contextual Design: Defining Customer Centered Systems* and *Rapid Contextual Design,* are used by companies and universities worldwide. As a member of ACM CHI (the association for computer-human interaction), Karen was awarded membership to the CHI Academy, a gathering of significant contributors, and received the first Lifetime Award for Practice, presented to her in 2010, for her impact on the field.

Karen has more than 25 years of teaching experience, both professionally and in university settings. She holds a doctorate in applied psychology from the University of Toronto.

Hugh Beyer has more than 20 years of experience building and designing applications, systems, and tools. He is co-founder of InContext Design, a user-centered design firm using Contextual Design's user-centered techniques to deliver data and design solutions with client teams across multiple industries. Hugh has designed solutions in the automotive, health care, security, call center, financial, and insurance industries.

Hugh provides the technical expertise and Agile know-how behind InContext's offerings. He works closely with clients' engineering and design teams to mesh often opposing points of view and build innovative solutions in virtually any development environment. Hugh's extensive understanding of the unique and varied capabilities of a wide range of technical platforms enables InContext to design innovative solutions. Hugh also works directly with InContext's design teams and coaches client teams in the Contextual Design process. He has pioneered the integration of customer-centered techniques into traditional development, using them to supercharge the Rational Unified Process, object-oriented design, and Agile. Hugh is the co-author of *Contextual Design: Defining Customer Centered Systems* which is used by companies and universities worldwide. Hugh's latest publication is *User-Centered Agile Methods*, which bridges the gap between the Agile development and UX communities.

Before co-founding InContext, Hugh acted as lead developer and architect in a range of systems at Digital Equipment Corp. His domains of experience include object-oriented repositories, databases, and integrated software development environments. Since starting InContext, Hugh has overseen the design of applications from desktop to Web to mobile, and from enterprise to small business to consumers in the wide variety of industries supported by InContext.

He holds a B.S. degree in applied mathematics from Harvard.

Printed in the United States
by Baker & Taylor Publisher Services